AA

MORE SHORT WALKS
— TO —
COUNTRY PUBS

100 Circular Walks to 100 Delightful Pubs
Includes Walks and Pubs in Scotland and Wales

First published March1994
© The Automobile Association 1994.
Assessments of walks and pubs are based on the editor's and
researchers' own experiences at the time of writing and
therefore this guide necessarily contains an element of
subjective opinion which may not reflect publishers' opinion
or dictate a reader's own opinion on another occasion. We
have tried to ensure accuracy in this guide but things do
change and we would be grateful if readers would advise us of
any inaccuracies they may encounter.

The contents of this publication are believed correct at the time
of printing. Nevertheless ,the publishers cannot be held
responsible for any errors or omissions or for changes in the
details given in this guide or for the consequences of any
reliance on the information provided by the same.

Walks devised and edited by David Hancock

Additional research by Vic Bates, Colin and Barbara Chase,
Steve and Fran Dunford, Derek Emmott, Dominic Goldberg,
Tony and Jean Gristock, Derek and Evelyn Hancock, Shiona
Hardie, Charles Hobbs, Janice Murray, Richard and Sally
Rhodes, Ron Smith, Bert Tasker, Bonita Toms

Illustrations by KAG Design
Filmset by Anton Graphics Ltd
Printed by BPCC Wheatons Ltd, Exeter

A CIP catalogue record for this book is available from the
British Library
ISBN 07495 0810 8   AA Ref. 11138

Published by AA Publishing, a trading name of Automobile
Association Developments Limited, whose registered office is
Norfolk House, Priestley Road, Basingstoke, Hampshire RG24
9NY. Registered number 1878835

$\mathscr{C}$ONTENTS

$\mathscr{J}$NTRODUCTION

USING THE GUIDE

Following the success of the first volume of Short Walks to Country Pubs, originally published in 1991, this second volume of walks introduces about 100 new pubs and walks and includes chapters on Wales and Scotland.

We have made every effort to ensure that the descriptions of the walks and the pubs are correct, but we can accept no liability for errors or omissions or for any consequences arising from them. Despite our best efforts to ensure accuracy, changes may occur at any stage during the lifetime of the book

THE PUBS

Each pub (bar three which are start points), forms the midpoint of a walk and has a short description intended to convey its character, the sort of food you may find, the hours when bar food is served and the beers and ciders on draught. All these details may change at short notice, and the information should be taken as a guide only. If you are walking with young children or a dog, do telephone in advance to check any restrictions there may be.

THE WALKS

The walks, mostly round trips, have been carefully chosen to take you through attractive and varied areas of countryside, to be enjoyable both for experienced and occasional walkers,

and to average about five miles in total. The approximate distance is always stated, but the time it will take to do the walk will vary considerably with the individual and the type of terrain. Generally, you should think in terms of two miles per hour, so the average five-mile walk would take two-and-a-half hours, excluding the visit to the pub. If the walk includes any particularly steep, muddy or difficult stretches, this is indicated in the brief characterisation under the distance.

DIRECTIONS AND MAPS

Route directions are as detailed as we can make them, but we believe it is essential to take the appropriate large-scale walkers' map with you - for example the Ordnance Survey Land ranger series (scale 1:50 000) is ideal, and we give the appropriate map sheet number and grid reference under the heading 'Parking', where appropriate, or 'Start of Walk' where no parking place can be specially highlighted. Paths and tracks followed by the walk are all marked on these maps and if by any chance you should miss your way, or need to make a detour because of temporary obstruction to a path, you will need such a map to re-orient yourself.

PARKING

Wherever possible our researchers have tried to recommend a place where you may be able to park. Sometimes it has not been possible to pick out a particular spot, and in these cases we have offered no information. Our suggestions are not a guarantee of any right to leave a vehicle parked. Please remember that it is your individual responsibility to ensure that your vehicle is safely parked, does not cause any obstruction to traffic or to access to a drive, field, or public or private building, and is not illegally using private land.

⊷CLOTHING⊶

You will need footwear such as light walking boots or well-fitting wellingtons with a good sole that will withstand wet and possibly muddy conditions. Remember that British weather is notoriously changeable, and on most days you may need a waterproof jacket and a sweater in case it turns cold.

PUBLIC FOOTPATHS, RIGHTS OF WAY, ⊷THE COUNTRY CODE⊶

Our routes follow public rights of way and established paths, tracks and bridleways wherever possible, but the routes sometimes include stretches along a road. Even country lanes can be deceptively busy, so keep

children and dogs close to you and walk so that you can see approaching traffic in good time.

Keep dogs on a lead if there are farm animals about - your pet may be reliable and unlikely to chase or bite, but farm animals, especially if they have young, can take violent exception to dogs they do not know.

When using a public path, you should encounter nothing more alarming than cattle, sheep or horses, but in some circumstances landowners have the right to put a bull in a field crossed by a public footpath. It is often said that a bull with a herd of cows is no threat, but as a general rule it is best to assume that bulls are completely unpredictable and take no chances.

Do keep to designated paths, and if you come to a crop field, go round the edge, not through the crops. If you open a gate, please remember to close it properly. Do not discard cans, bags, bottles or food because these are a danger to farm animals as well as an eyesore to everyone else. If you do find that a public path has been obstructed, it is better to tell the Rights of Way Officer in the Highways and Traffic Department of the local county council than to try to argue or force your way through.

The Chequers at Thompson in Norfolk

*M*OUSEHOLE ~to~ *L*AMORNA

**APPROXIMATELY
5 MILES**

A peaceful walk across fields and through old farmsteads, returning along the undulating cliff path, abundant with wild flowers in early summer. Some tricky descents and a steep climb.

Parking
OS Map 203 Ref SW4726. Pay and display car parks, harbour and edge of village towards Newlyn.

Lamorna Wink
Lamorna, near Penzance. Off B3315 3½ mile south- west of Penzance.

FURTHER EXPLORATION

Mousehole
The most picturesque of Cornish fishing villages, with narrow lanes and passageways flanked by traditional granite cottages and encircling a charming harbour.

Lamorna Cove
A beautiful little cove with remnants of a granite quarry on one side, which supplied stone to build the Thames Embankment and several

*W*alk beside the harbour, passing the Ship Inn, then wend your way up the main street to pass the Wesleyan chapel before ascending steeply out of the village. Veer sharp right with the lane, ignoring the coast path sign off to the left, and continue along the road to reach Raginnis Farm on your right. Take the waymarked path opposite the farm and bear half-right across pasture, then follow the defined path through four fields keeping to the right. Good views left across Mounts Bay to St Michael's Mount and the Lizard. On reaching Kemyel Farm keep the first barn (opposite the farm house) to your left, pass through a small gate, then climb a series of stiles to skirt the farm buildings to meet a stony track. Bear left, and follow the footpath round to the right. Continue along what can be an overgrown path, over an easily missed small river that flows under some boulders, through a field and out into a lane. Keep left past Kemyel Crease Farm, traverse three fields to join another track, then pass through the farm buildings to where the track forks. Keep left passing a house on the right to enter a field, then bear diagonally left over a stile onto a narrow footpath which wends its way up the Lamorna valley eventually leading you to the road at the top of the valley. Turn left and proceed past the pretty old mill and its small waterfall to the pub.

∽*Lamorna Wink* (Devenish)∾

A traditional, simply furnished village local only a few minutes stroll from the pretty cove. The stone-floored bar houses a fine collection of well kept naval memorabilia and pictures. The Wink was originally only licensed to sell beer, but a 'wink' to the landlord would produce something a little stronger, probably some smuggled liquor. Children's room.

On draught: Boddingtons Bitter, Flowers Original, Marston's Pedigree, Stella Artois.

Food: decent snacks include filled baked potatoes, local pasties, sandwiches (from £1.20), ploughman's (£3.25) or fisherman's lunch (£3.75).

Times: 11am-2.30pm and 6-9pm, Sun 12-2.30pm and 7-9pm. Telephone: 0736 731566.

———————

From the pub follow the valley road down into Lamorna Cove. Take the left-hand path up towards the cliff path, then at a footpath waymarker and a fork of routes, keep right to join the coastal path. The approximate 2½ mile walk back to Mousehole along the coastal path is very pretty, and during the summer months there is an abundance of wild flowers. It also passes through the wooded Kemyel Crease Nature Reserve. The path is rocky in places and there is a fairly steep climb towards the end, before emerging at the top of the hill looking down over Mousehole. Retrace steps downhill back into the harbour.

lighthouses, including Longships and Wolf Rock . The manager's house and chapel are now the Lamorna Cove Hotel.

Merry Maidens Stone Circle

A circle of 19 stones ¾ mile off B3315 - said to be a group of girls turned to stone as a punishment for dancing on the Sabbath. Nearby stones are said to represent the musicians who played for them.

Minack Theatre, Porthcurno

A spectacular Greek-style amphitheatre hewn out of the cliffs high above the sea. There are evening performances in summer and Minack can be viewed (entrance charge) during the day.

ALTARNUN CIRCULAR WALK

**APPROXIMATELY
5½ MILES**

*A peaceful undulating
ramble across scenic
field paths through the
parish of Altarnun -
the largest parish in
Cornwall - affording
good views of the
northern edge of
Bodmin Moor. Can be
wet and muddy in
places.*

Locate the post office and take waymarked path
Tresmaine - through gate, barn-yard and over a
stile. Head uphill, climb a stile, bear half-left to gate
and keep to left-hand hedge to gate and stile and enter
Tresmaine Farm. Bear left along drive, signed Oldhay
go through gate, then at sharp left bend, proceed
through gate ahead and bear diagonally left across
pasture to a wall stile. Keep left along field edge, climb
stile, bear left across field, through a gap in hedge and
head left downhill to a gate. Proceed across to hedge
keep right through an old gateway to two gates and
pass through the left-hand gate. Head downhill around
Oldhay Farm, then continue steeply downhill to a wall
stile and cross pasture to footbridge. Follow defined
path uphill to Tresnarrett Farm, turning left (arrow)
along field edge to stile in corner. Cross further stile by
telegraph pole, proceed across pasture to obscured stile
in hedge, then cross a brook and head uphill to stile
beside a pole fence. Keep right of small barn, bear left
and pass through gates into
Trebullom Farm, following
driveway to lane. Turn
left, then where lane
veers left, turn right
on to sunken track
to a lane. Turn
right, then left
at T-junction
for ½ mile
to pub.

◇ *Rising Sun (Free House)* ◇

Originally a farmhouse operating 30 acres, this 16th-century pub enjoys an unspoilt and remote setting on the fringe of Bodmin Moor. The rather run-down exterior appearance belies the true rustic and lively atmosphere that fills the character, flagstoned main bar, complete with open log fire. Children welcome in family room. Overnight accommodation.

On draught: a changing selection of ales may include Flowers Original, Bateman XB, Cotleigh Tawny, Bass, Heineken, Stella Artois, Dry Blackthorn cider.

Food: a comprehensive good value bar menu lists soup (£1.50), cod and chips (£3.50), sandwiches (from £1.30), moussaka (£4), meat pie (£4.50) and ploughman's (from £2.50). Puddings include fruit pie and sponge and custard (£1). Hearty daily specials range from seafood pie to beef in Guinness. Traditional Sunday lunch (£3.80).

Times: 12-2.30pm and 6.30-9.45pm. Telephone: 0566 86636.

————◆◆◆◆————

urn right from the pub and follow lane, keeping ahead at crossroads towards South Carne. Cross river bridge, bear left uphill shortly to turn left along drive to Tresmeake Farm. Pass through farmyard and gate on to muddy track to two further gates. Go through left-hand gate, keep right-handed across two fields and bear half-right across third pasture to gate and brook. Continue straight ahead to a gate, turn left along lane passing farm, then bear right on to waymarked track in front of house to a gate. Proceed downhill into field, bear left with arrow, keeping ahead near gate through scrub to stile. Keep left, cross footbridge, a stile and bear half-left to wall stile. Proceed right-handed to a stile and from here follow waymarkers across stiles and through gates to a lane leading to A30. Turn left, then shortly left again on to path waymarked Altarnun. On reaching a lane turn left back into the village.

Parking
OS Map 201 Ref SX2182.
Centre of Altarnun village, one mile north of A30.

Rising Sun
Altarnun, near Launceston. One mile north of the village on the Five Lanes to Camelford road (well signposted).

FURTHER EXPLORATION

Altarnun
A moorland village above a stream on the edge of Bodmin Moor and Cornwall's largest parish. Two little streams, crossed by a ford and a narrow bridge, flow through the village past the uneven stone walls of cottages. The large 15th-century church of St Nonna, known locally as the 'cathedral of the moor' has an imposing tower and a profusion of handsomely carved bench-ends.

Trewint
John Wesley, founder of Methodism, spent some time in a small cottage here between 1744 and 1762. The cottage, restored in 1950, has been turned into a shrine to his memory and a Wesley Day service is held here annually.

$\mathcal{P}$ETER TAVY ~to~ $\mathcal{H}$ORNDON

**APPROXIMATELY
5 MILES**

*This walk explores
field paths, moorland
tracks and the Tavy
valley on the western
fringes of Dartmoor
and affords magnifi-
cent moorland views.
Look out for soaring
buzzards and dippers
along the River Tavy.*

$\mathcal{T}$urn left uphill away from the church and soon take the first narrow metalled lane right, following it uphill across a cattle grid and on past two houses. Pass a small parking area, then shortly bear off left, waymarked White Tor, onto a wide stony track and proceed uphill. Where the track levels bear left along a defined grassy track lined with a row of stones to a metal gate. Keep left-handed across rock-strewn pasture and begin to descend to a wooden gate in the field corner. Beyond, follow the tree-lined bank downhill to join a stony path to a gate, then follow it to a narrow farm road. Turn left, walk downhill through the hamlet of Cudliptown to a quiet lane and turn right. In about half-a-mile at an old milestone on your left, turn left to join an ancient stony track that heads downhill into the Tavy valley. Cross the river bridge and gradually ascend out of the valley, where the track becomes metalled and enters Horndon. At a fork of lanes keep left, then at a T-junction turn left for the inn.

ᗏ*Elephant's Nest (Free House)*ᗐ

Sixteenth-century miners' cottages form the nucleus of this isolated inn, with various rooms featuring stone walls, slate floors, open fires and an array of pine tables, wall pews, stools and country chairs. To the front is an attractive lawned garden with picnic benches and glorious views across unspoilt countryside. Children are welcome inside away from the main bar. There are two guest bedrooms available.

On draught: good range of changing ales such as St Austell Hicks Special, Dorset Best Bitter, Greene King IPA, Palmers IPA, Murphy's and Guinness. Food: a blackboard menu offers home-made soup (£1.30), Wiltshire ham bake (£3.90), local game pie (£5), elephant's lunch (£3.30), ploughman's from £2.80 and for pudding the choice includes treacle and walnut tart and steamed apple and date sponge.

Times: 11.30am (12 Sun)-2pm and 6.30 (7 Sun)-10pm.
Telephone: 0822 810273.

From the far corner of the inn car park, pass through a gap in the hedge onto a track. Go downhill to where it bears left, cross a stile at a footpath sign and follow a path to another wall-stile, then bear left (yellow arrow) along a track to a wooden gate. Keep right along the edge of pasture, uphill with the yellow markers to a fence stile by a gate, then go half-left across a field to climb a wall stile in the far left corner. Keep left-handed along the hedge, climb another wall stile, bear diagonally left and join a track that keeps left of a stone building to a ladder stile. A path follows the right-hand field edge towards Mary Tavy church, then at a gate turn left with the fingerpost to follow the field edge to go through a further gate and turn right. Keep right to a wall stile, cross to the main gate of the churchyard. Turn left along the lane and keep left at the National Power sign on a waymarked bridlepath to Peter Tavy. Head downhill, cross the river footbridge and follow the path along the valley side, through a wooden gate and along a path which takes you back to the church in Peter Tavy.

Start of walk
OS Map 201 Ref SX5177.
Beside church.

Elephant's Nest
Horndon, Mary Tavy, Tavistock.
The pub is signposted off A386
at Mary Tavy.

FURTHER EXPLORATION

Lydford
This village once had a royal mint and the Castle Inn has four silver 'Lydford Pennies'. The real castle is said to be haunted by Judge Jeffries, amongst others. The spectacular gorge (NT) of the River Lyd features the White Lady Waterfall.

Brentor
North of Peter Tavy this 1,100 ft cone of volcanic rock is topped by the medieval Church of St Michael.

ᴍORETONHAMPSTEAD ~to~ ɴORTH BOVEY

**APPROXIMATELY
4 MILES**

*An enjoyable
undulating ramble
along a network of
paths, tracks and a
quiet country lane on
the fringes of
Dartmoor. Superb
open views across
moorland and vale
with the opportunity
to see buzzards.*

Parking
OS Map 191 Ref SX8675 Free
car park on B3212 on the west
side of Moretonhampstead.

Ring of Bells
Village Square, North Bovey.
Off B3212, two miles west of
Moretonhampstead.

FURTHER EXPLORATION

North Bovey
With its old thatched cottages
around the village green, many
consider this to be Devon's
most picturesque village.

From the car park turn left into the village then take the first right - Pound Street - (sp North Bovey). Where it bears sharp right for the village, keep ahead down a narrow lane passing Pound Cottage. Cross a brook and ascend past the drive to Brinning, before climbing a stile, left, signed North Bovey via Narramore and Fursdon. Follow a grassy track into pasture, then left-handed uphill to a stile by an old gateway and maintain direction along a field edge, across a green lane and pasture beyond to a stile. Bear right on a path through a group of trees with Narramore farm to the left to a stile into a paddock. Cross the paddock and a further stile, then bear right along the drive to a lane and straight across to join a signed track beyond a gate. Follow this towards Fursdon Farm, then at a fingerpost climb a stile on your right to cross pasture to a further stile and cross the farm drive. Pass through a gate, bear left with the signpost to cross a ladder stile and proceed, with the farm to your left, to a wooden gate. A sign points you downhill to a stile in the hedge, then cross a brook and head across a field to a gate between two trees. Cross the stile, keep left-handed along a hedge, downhill to a stile and join a track into the valley bottom. Cross stile, turn right by barn and follow bridleway to pub.

⊷*Ring O'Bells* (*Free House*)⊶

This delightful thatched 13th-century inn stands close to the green in a picturesque Dartmoor village. Thick walls, low ceilings, and huge inglenook fireplaces characterise the interior. There is a garden, an attractive restaurant and overnight accommodation is available. Children welcome.

On draught: changing ales may include Wadworth 6X, Dartmoor Best Bitter, Marston's Pedigree, Guinness, and Carlsberg Export. **Food:** popular bar food features farmhouse pâté (£2.95), fresh sardines (£3.25), steak and kidney pie (£5.95), chilli (£4.25), vegetable pie (£5.25), roast half pheasant (£8.50), fillet of cod (£7.50). **Times:** 12-2pm and 6.30-9pm. Telephone: 0647 40375.

From the pub turn right, pass the village hall and at junction keep right uphill to where the lane turns sharp right. Bear off left onto a lane and look for a fence stile ('footpath' written on it) to your right. Bear half-left across a field to a stile, then diagonally right uphill to a gate in the left corner of pasture. Turn left (signed), pass through a gate and continue to a stile in the wall. Turn right onto a lane, then almost immediately left onto a waymarked track. Go through a gate, then keep left-handed in pasture following yellow markers through two metal gates to a track across a field to a gate. Continue to a barn, bear left (signed), then shortly right (waymarked) through a gate and downhill across a field to a stile by a gate. Keep right-handed steeply downhill, bearing right to a stile and brook and join a lane that climbs uphill to join B3212. Turn right and the car park will be on your left.

Becky Falls
(3 miles south)
Set in glorious woodland, the falls cascade over huge granite boulders

Castle Drogo
This imposing castle stands on a crag above the River Teign, with wonderful views. National Trust. Telephone: 0647 33306.

$\mathcal{S}$HORT WALK ~from~ $\mathcal{B}$URGH ISLAND

APPROXIMATELY 5½ MILES

This peaceful varied walk begins and finishes at the beach car park opposite Burgh Island and its fascinating pub. Tracks and the coast path afford fine views along the South Devon coast and Avon estuary. (The sea tractor crosses on the hour at the time of writing, but check). The distance is 300 yards

Parking
OS Map 202 Ref SX6646
Beach car park (charge) at
Bigbury-on -Sea.

Pilchard Inn
Burgh Island, Bigbury-on-Sea.
Signposted off A379
Kingsbridge to Modbury road.

$\mathcal{H}$ead west to pick up the coast path, signed to Challaborough. Walk along Marine Drive to where Ringmere Drive bears off right and follow coast path into Challaborough. Pass in front of caravan park, then bear left onto the coast path waymarked Aymer Cove. At a swing gate leave the coast path to follow a narrow path inland, then along a field edge to a gate near a bungalow, Follow a track into Ringmore, bearing left onto the village lane. Turn right beyond the post office onto a grass-centred track to a stile and gate. Bear diagonally left downhill (waymarked) across pasture to a stile in the far corner, then half-right to a gate in the valley bottom. Follow the grassy path to an arrowed post, turn right over a brook onto a track, then shortly turn left, recrossing the brook, and through a gate. Head uphill on a high- banked lane to a metalled lane. Turn left uphill to Bigbury Green then right along the B-road. Where this bears sharp right, keep straight on along a waymarked metalled lane which becomes a track down towards the Avon estuary, passing a large white house to a gate. Pass Newquay Cottage, turn right onto a signed path and head uphill through a gate, out of the valley towards Hexdown Farm. Cross the farmyard via a series of gates and follow the main drive (waymarked) uphill to a T-junction of metalled tracks opposite the golf course. Turn left, then once on the course turn right (yellow arrow) beyond a group of fir trees and cross the tee, keeping left-handed to a stile on the perimeter corner of the course. Follow telegraph poles to a stile and lane, turn left, then shortly turn right, opposite a farm entrance, onto a signed footpath through large gates onto a shale track that heads uphill to a gate and junction of paths. Turn left, pass through a gate beside an old water tank and proceed downhill to a stile and enter Bigbury-on-Sea. Head downhill back to the beach car park and Burgh Island . At high tide wait for the tractor, or summon it by phoning the pub from the phone box on the lane.

⊖*Pilchard Inn* (*Free House*)⊙

This atmospheric 14th-century smugglers' pub boasts a superb island location with glorious views along the beautiful Devon coastline. The two tiny beamed bars are unspoilt with lots of bare wood and stone, a variety of rustic tables, settles and chairs and a warming open fire for those wild windy winter days. Picnic benches on the terrace below are popular in summer months. Children are welcome in the lower eating area but not in the bars upstairs.

On draught: Wadworth 6X (winter), Ushers Best Bitter (summer), Carlsberg, Holsten, Taunton Traditional cider. **Food:** choices include a selection of ploughman's, filled French sticks, salads from £3.50, a range of filled jacket potatoes from £2.25 and chilli for £4.25. It can get very busy at the height of the season. **Times:** food is served throughout the day, from midday to 9pm, Etr - Oct only. Telephone: 0548 810344.

FURTHER EXPLORATION

Burgh Island
The island's Art Deco hotel, setting for one of Agatha Christie's mysteries, 'Evil Under the Sun', is even more famous than the Pilchard. Built by an eccentric millionaire in 1929, the hotel became an exclusive retreat for the rich and famous, including, at various times, Noel Coward, the Duke of Windsor and Mrs Simpson, Kirk Douglas and the Beatles. Agatha Christie wrote six of her books while staying here.

£XMINSTER ~to~ ℃URF

APPROXIMATELY 4 MILES

A short walk exploring the banks of the Exeter Canal, the Exe estuary and surrounding meadowland. Bring your binoculars as the estuary is a prime birdwatching area - especially renpwnefor waders and ducks.

Parking

OS Map SX192 Ref 9487. Free car park by the village hall in Exminster.

Turf

Turf Lock, Exminster. South of village off A379. Take lane past Swans Nest to end of track and car park, then walk along canal to pub.

FURTHER EXPLORATION

Exminster

Located on the west bank of the Exe the town has fine views over the valley to To Topsham. The church is one of the county's earliest minsters

*L*eave your car, turn right along the main village road passing some shops, then turn right into Milbury Lane opposite the primary school. Remain on the lane out of the village and go across the bridges over the A379 and railway. The metalled lane gives way to a track and where this bears sharp left, keep ahead at footpath sign and cross a stile into pasture. Proceed straight on, the defined grassy path running parallel with a dyke across lush meadowland towards the canal bank and Topsham church ahead. Eventually, climb a stile and a reed-fringed channel and shortly bear right along a grass-centred track which leads you up onto the bank of the Exeter Canal. Follow the narrow towpath south, arrowed to The Turf (1m). This delightful path affords good all-round views and later across the widening expanse of the Exe estuary. At the end of the path cross the canal lock to the Turf Hotel.

☙*Turf Hotel* (Free House) ❧

Gloriously located where the canal enters the Exe estuary, the Turf enjoys superb views down the river from its large riverside garden - complete with barbecue, children's playhouse and birdwatching hide - and from the bay windows of the bright airy and relaxing bars. The three rooms have bare floorboards laid out with old and modern farmhouse chairs and various local paintings and bird prints decorate the walls. Overnight accommodation is available and children are very welcome.

On draught: Wadworth 6X, Boddingtons Bitter, Flowers Original, Exe Valley Bitter, Stella Artois, Heineken, Dry Blackthorn cider.
Food: the blackboard menu may feature chilli and tacos (£4.25), home-cooked ham platter (£4.95), lasagne with garlic bread (£5.50), various ploughman's and sandwiches and a soup such as leek and tomato or carrot, apple and cashew nut for £1.95. Puddings

include treacle pudding and sticky toffee pudding for £2. A choice of curries is available on Friday evenings, cream teas on summer afternoons.

Times: 12-2pm and 6-9pm (Sun from 7pm). Telephone: 0392 833128.

From the Turf recross the lockgate, bear right, then at the footpath fingerpost turn left and drop down off the towpath onto a stony track and cross the small footbridge and stile in front of you. Bear half-right with the grassy path and cross pasture to a stile beside a gate. Go over a dyke and a further stile, then head diagonally left across the meadow on a defined path towards the railway line. A yellow arrow waymarks the route as you negotiate a few tiny footbridges over drainage ditches. Eventually, walk parallel to the railway, climb two stiles (arrows) and maintain direction to where the route becomes a grassy track beside the railway. Pass through a large white gate, turn right along a tarmacked lane, then where this merges with another lane bear sharp left and cross the bridge over the railway. Walk past the Swan's Nest pub and follow the footway to the roundabout at the end of the lane. Cross over A379 (care needed) to follow the lane into Exminster village and the village hall car park.

and has connections with St Boniface. The peal of eight bells ringing out from the church tower is one of the finest in Devon.

Powderham Castle - (3m south-east)

The estate fringes the shore of the estuary and has been the home of the Courtneys, Earls of Devon, since 1390. The original building was transformed by a major 18th-century reconstruction. The somewhat flamboyantly decorated rooms are beautifully furnished and well worth a visit.

$\mathcal{S}$TOKE SUB HAMDON ~to~ $\mathcal{M}$ONTACUTE

$\mathcal{L}$eave the car park, turn right up the hill, then on reaching a cattle grid bear right onto the marked bridleway across the common and through the wood (ignore cross-paths) to reach. Turn right and after 100 yards go left up a steep path, signed Ham Hill. Where tracks cross at the top of the climb, turn right along the ridge to reach a crossroads of tracks by a wooded dell. Turn left (Liberty Trail), and at a T-junction turn right downhill. At the bottom, just before a lane, leave Liberty Trail, turn sharp left over a stile and head gradually back uphill to follow the wire fence on the right. Beyond a stile the path bears slightly right and steepens to reach a track leading to a road near some barns. Cross the road onto a footpath (Hedgecock Lane) which runs parallel to the road below. On reaching the village outskirts rejoin the road soon to turn left along a gravel lane past the pond to the church. Turn right at the main road for the pub.

$\backsim$*Phelips Arms (Palmers)*$\backsim$

Overlooking 'The Borough' or central square, this is one of the many beautiful old two-storey ham-stone houses with typical mullioned windows which surround it. The one spacious bar is comfortably furnished and a huge stone fireplace adds character There are newspapers to read and overnight accommodation is available. Outside is a tranquil walled garden with flower borders. No children or dogs are allowed inside.

On draught: Palmers Bridport Bitter, IPA, Guinness, Labatts, Kronenbourg, Dry Blackthorn cider. **Food:** a wide menu includes soup (£1.50), chilli beef tostada, broccoli and cream cheese bake and herby lamb pie (£4.75), 10oz sirloin steak (£7.75), chicken curry (£4.75), and various salads (from £4.50). Puddings include treacle tart, chocolate rum mousse (both £1.75).

Times: 12-2pm and 6-10pm. Telephone: 0935 822557.

*R*etrace your steps to the church. Go left up the no through road, then take the path right through Abbey Farm forecourt, signed Hedgecock Hill Wood. Exit via a gate and follow the track past the wood on the right and across the meadow to a stile and woods opposite. Shortly, fork left and continue via stiles marked with yellow arrows. The path levels out for some distance, then on an unmarked merging of trails drop down to a lower level where the path resumes its direction. Cross the path marked to East Stoke, shortly to climb the steps to the Prince of Wales pub. (If you emerge from the wood higher up, the pub is easy to see). Keep to its right on the tarmac road and enter old quarry workings. From a high point locate the pinnacle of the War Memorial at the far side and make your way there. Find the path marked Highway, but do not take it. Turn left and take the unmarked path down to the road and car park, which can be seen below.

Montacute House (National Trust)

The 17th-century house has many fine interior features. Collections include some splendid Elizabethan and Jacobean portraits in the Long Gallery. Garden and park open all year; house Apr-Oct daily (except Tue). Telephone: 0935 823289.

ℒYDEARD HILL ~to~ 𝒯RISCOMBE

APPROXIMATELY
4½ MILES

Generally an easy walk, although there is one very steep climb out of Triscombe requiring stout shoes, especially in wet weather. The reward is a superb view from the highest point on the Quantocks - Will's Neck - from which, on a clear day, three National Parks are visible: Dartmoor, Exmoor and the Brecon Beacons.

From the car park take the main stony track north-west following the wire fence on your left for half a mile until you come to a stile in a belt of trees. Beyond the stile, turn left onto a track which leads down to West Bagborough. At the village street turn right, then shortly right again through the lych-gate, waymarked Rock Farm. Turn left near the church and walk past the walled garden, through a kissing gate and then along the right-hand edge of fields until you reach a barn. Go through the gate, then immediately right through another gate and follow the path across three gated fields towards a farmhouse. Beyond the third metal gate, leave the main track to the house and keep straight ahead over rough pasture to a stile in the hedge and cross the last field to a lane. Turn right past the farm and proceed up the track to a gate, then take the left fork and follow the path along the woodland edge to a road. Turn right for the pub.

❧*Blue Ball Inn (Free House)*❧

Sheltered in the arms of wooded hills this isolated thatched inn was once a row of cottages and first licensed to sell ale in 1766. Its stone façade is softened by colourful flowers and shrubs and the garden is a delightful series of terraced lawns. Low, heavily beamed ceilings, a huge inglenook, sturdy oak tables, settles and other rustic furniture characterise the thick-walled bar. The attractive front conservatory is ideal for children.

On draught: Exmoor Ale, Cotleigh Tawny, guest ales, Guinness, Castlemaine XXXX, Lowenbrau, Dry Blackthorn cider, Gaymers Olde English cider. Food: the seasonally changing menu may feature lentil bake (£5.25), broccoli and cheese quiche (£3.95), chilli (£4.95), steak and kidney pie (£5.25), chicken breast Cajun-style (£5.85) and poached salmon Hollandaise (£6.50). Snacks include sandwiches, filled jacket potatoes (from £2) and a choice of ploughman's (£3.25). Savoury and sweet pancakes are a speciality and puddings like Somerset apple cake and raspberry and redcurrant pie are popular.

Times: 12-2pm and 7-9pm. Telephone: 09848 242.

---

*T*urn right from the pub up the Bagborough road to where the outward footpath joined the road, then turn sharp left onto a footpath back round the hill until the pub is visible below, through the trees. Here turn right up a very steep earth bank on a less well defined path. The path becomes stony then grassy as it becomes less steep and trees and bracken gives way to bilberries and heather. Keep going to the top, with views from Bridgwater Bay to the Mendips and across the Bristol Channel to Wales, and the coast back as far as Minehead. Continue past the trig point along the ridge, an ancient drove road known as King Alfred's Way. Close by, barrows mark the graves of Bronze Age people who may also have used this track. Descending gradually, carry on past a wood on your right and continue until you reach the stile and track back to your car.

Parking
OS Map 181 Ref ST1833. Free car park on Lydeard Hill, 1 mile north-east of West Bagborough.

Blue Ball Inn
Triscombe. Three-quarters of a mile off A358 Taunton to Minehead road.

FURTHER EXPLORATION

Coleridge Cottage
Nether Stowey (National Trust) The house in which Coleridge wrote 'The Ancient Mariner'. Telephone: 0278 732662.

West Somerset Railway
Britains longest preserved railway from Minehead to Bishop's Lydeard. Telephone: 0643 704996. Talking Timetable: 0643 707650.

⚓ITTLETON-UPON-SEVERN ~to~ OLDBURY-ON-SEVERN

APPROXIMATELY 5 MILES

An undemanding walk, much of it along the dyke built by Dutch engineers in the 17th century to help reclaim land from the Severn. Good views of the Severn Bridge and across the saltings where men still catch salmon with nets.

Parking
OS Maps 162/172 Ref ST5989. Main street near Post Office in Littleton-upon- Severn.

Anchor Inn
Church Road, Oldbury-on-Severn. Two miles north-west of Thornbury, off B4061.

FURTHER EXPLORATION

Oldbury Church
Built on a hill south of the village and a landmark on this walk.

*G*o along the no-through-road beside the Post Office, following the track for three-quarters of a mile. Do not enter the field ahead but turn right,then immediately left through a gate to join a hedged grassy track. At the next gate bear half-right across a meadow to a stile in the right-hand corner, then cross and turn right along Littleton Warth. Follow the dyke for about two miles to an inlet opposite the clubhouse for Thornbury Yacht Club. Continue round to the right but do not go over the sluice, instead leave the dyke and follow the fence on your right. Cross a paddock via stiles and continue along the track past Oldbury Riding School to the road. Turn left for the pub.

⊷*Anchor* (Free House)⊷

Built in the 17th century on the site of an old mill house, this mellow stone, wisteria-clad building became a pub during the village's seafaring days, when barges pulled up alongside it. The old waterway can still be seen, although much of it is overgrown. Inside, the main split-level lounge bar is dominated by a wide inglenook fireplace and furnished with an assortment of comfortable chairs and tables. A large sunny garden with benches features a pétanque pitch. Children are welcome in the dining area.

On draught: Bass, Marston's Pedigree, Theakston Best and Old Peculier, Butcombe Bitter, Guinness, Newquay Steam Pils, Blands West Country cider.
Food: generous helpings of home-cooked food, include Mexican beef (£4.75), pork Normandy (£4.85), lasagne (£3.95), Oldbury Flat Hat - roast beef and Yorkshire Pud (£4.10) and popular salads (from £2.95). Desserts range from caramel apple granny to blackcurrant supreme (£2.10).
Times: 11.30am-2pm and 6.30-9pm (6pm Sat), Sun 12-2pm and 7-9.30pm. Telephone: 0454 413331

*T*urn left on leaving the pub, then shortly right along Westmarsh Lane. Where the tarmac ends, take the grassy track ahead to reach a lane. Turn right and immediately after Cowhill Cider House take the footpath right, waymarked Littleton, between the houses. Enter the overgrown orchard and bear half-left to a hidden stile. Cross and continue along the left-hand hedge into a second field, then carry straight on and make for the gap in the hedge at the right of the wood ahead. Continue ahead on the track past the church and out to the lane. Turn right, then opposite Corston Farm go left through a farm gate and cross the field to a stile, just visible to the right of a wall. Beyond the stile, turn right onto the track, then left at the road back to your car.

Oldbury Power Station -
One of three nuclear power stations on the Severn. There are tours daily. Closed Sat Oct to Mar.

Oldown Farm and Forest
(South-east of Littleton off B4461)
Gardens, animals, adventure playground, shop and restaurant. Closed Mon, except Bank Hols.
Telephone: 0454 413605.

ᛒURRINGTON ~to~ CHURCHILL

APPROXIMATELY 5 MILES

A cool shady outward walk takes you around the wooded slopes of Mendip Lodge Wood and Dolebury Warren. A steep climb on your return journey over Dolebury Warren, affords wonderful views. As well as an Iron Age hill fort, there are traces of a Celtic field system

Walk down past the Burrington Inn and opposite the garden centre cross to The Cottage where, to its left, look for a blue-painted railing and turn left up a well hidden footpath to reach a metalled lane. Turn left, then after 150 yards, turn right onto a woodland path. On reaching a ruin, proceed through the clearing ahead and maintain direction, passing more ruins before turning left onto a track to head uphill, shortly to cross a stile on your right (Woodland Trust). Take the right fork which after some distance brings you down to the woodland fringe. After passing a building on your left, you will reach two wooden gates, cross the stile by the left one and take the path past the cottages and through a gate into a fir plantation. After a stile, follow a garden hedge on the right until, at a right-hand bend, leave the main path and go ahead over some iron-bar steps into a meadow. Cross to a white gate by a bungalow to reach the road, then cross into Skinners Lane and follow it to the pub.

⟡ *Crown (Free House)* ⟡

This picturesque stone pub was once an old coaching stop, and at one time housed the village butcher and grocer's shops. Two atmospheric bars have slated and flagstoned floors, stone walls, heavy beams. open fires and various nooks and crannies with intimate seating. Delightful walled terrace and lawned front garden with tables and benches, plus a sheltered rear lawn. Children are welcome inside away from the bar and dogs are allowed in the front garden only, if on a lead.

On draught: Eldridge Pope Dorchester Bitter, Hardy Country, Palmers IPA, Butcombe Bitter, Bass, Batch Bitter (Cotleigh Harrier), up to four guest ales, Guinness, Murphy's, Labatts, Kronenbourg 1664, Dry Blackthorn, Long Ashton (local) cider.

Food: hearty pub fare includes 'Trenchers' - an enormous French stick with various fillings (from £3.20) - rare beef salad (£4.75), filled jacket potatoes (from £2.40), sandwiches (from £2) and daily hot dishes like cauliflower cheese (£3.75) or venison casserole (£5.25).

Times: 12-2pm (no food in evenings). Telephone: 0943 852995.

From the pub turn left uphill and shortly take the bridleway left down to the main road. Cross and go up Dolberrow opposite, passing some cottages. After a pink cottage, Dolberrow Rising, bear left onto a gated woodland path and follow this up to the Iron Age fort and the summit and continue along the grassy ridge. After a stile keep on the main track past pine trees then bear right, following yellow arrows (Limestone Link), then turn left downhill towards a distant house, to join a track beyond a stile. Turn right to a crossing of tracks, then keep left uphill to where Black Down Moor opens out on your right. Keep to the track along the woodland edge. It eventually becomes metalled and drops down to join the outward route. Take the footpath, right, back to the car park.

Parking
OS Map 172/182 Ref ST4758. Free car park at Burrington Combe on the B3134, next to the Burrington Inn.

Crown Inn
The Batch, Skinners Lane, Churchill, Bristol. Three miles south of Congresbury.

FURTHER EXPLORATION

Rock of Ages
(opposite car park) A deep cleft in the huge rocky outcrop provided inspiration to the author of the famous hymn during a storm in 1702.

Blagdon
(2 miles west of Burrington) Good views across Blagdon Lake from the Church of St Andrews, which has one of the county's tallest towers.

Cheddar Gorge
The most famous gorge and cave system in Britain. Open daily. Telephone: 0934 742343

ΒEAMINSTER ~to~ STOKE ABBOTT

**APPROXIMATELY
4½ MILES**

*An undulating ramble
past flower-filled
woods and riverbanks,
then onto bracing
Dorset hills with
grand views to tree-
clad Lewesdon Hill
and the coast.*

Parking
OS Map 193 Ref ST4701. Free
parking in the central square
by the market cross.

New Inn
Stoke Abbott, Beaminster. Off
B3162 Bridport to
Broadwindsor road.

FURTHER EXPLORATION

Parnham House
Beaminster
This fine Tudor mansion, with
14 acres of grounds, is the
home of John Makepeace's
furniture-making workshop,
which is open to visitors. There
are regular exhibitions. Open
Apr to Oct. Telephone: 0308
862204.

From the square go down Church Street, then left
along St Mary Well Street and up the no-through
road marked 'Bridleway to Netherbury', which
becomes a track leading to a cottage. Cross the stile to
the right, follow the river bank for quarter of a mile,
then bear slightly right past an old brick icehouse to a
track and gate. With the wood on your left soon reach
a stony farm track and turn right uphill for 200yds
before crossing the stile on your left. Head straight
across the field, then bear left to a stile in the lower
corner. Cross the stream and a stile, then turn right in
the meadow to another small bridge between two
stiles. Beyond these bear right to follow the contour
through several rough paddocks, keeping above the
stream on your right. Where wooden posts cross at
right angles, turn right and walk down between the
railings, jump the stream, and follow the woodland
path with the stream on your right. Ignore the path to
the left. Cross another small stream and leave the
woods by a stile. Head uphill to a gate in the hedge
and follow the grassy track for half a mile. Keep
straight on at the T-junction, then where the track turns
sharp left, take the narrow footpath to the right down a
steep gully to emerge opposite the church. Go up the
concrete lane past the church to the village road. Turn
right for the pub.

๑New Inn (Palmers)๑

This large, thatched, stone-built, 17th-century pub has
many brick-arched windows overlooking a peaceful
walled garden. The Thatch Bar is spacious with heavy
black beams studded with a collection of horsebrasses,
a massive inglenook fireplace and traditional furniture.
Children are welcome in the attractive dining room.
No dogs.
On draught: Palmers Bridport Bitter, IPA and Tally
Ho, Guinness, Castlemaine XXXX, Kronenbourg, Dry
Blackthorn cider.

Food: daily specials may include broccoli and cauliflower mornay (£3.10), gamekeeper's pie (£4.20), country fish pie, and chicken breast in garlic and coriander (both £4.75). There is also a range of ploughman's (from £3) and sandwiches with salad (from £1.80). Traditional Sunday roasts.

Times: 12-2pm and 7-9pm. Telephone: 0308 68333.

From the pub turn right up the lane and take the next left to Chart Knolle. On reaching the house pass through the yard, then turn right onto the bridlepath that runs along the back of the house to two gates. Go through the right-hand one, maintain direction across the left-hand edge of a paddock to another gate and proceed up the grassy path to the top of the tree-lined hill. From the top head down towards Beaminster, across a gated track in the corner of the field, and then descend steeply past a lone oak to the well defined track over the footbridge and head up the other side to a stile. Cross the field to the left of Higher Barrowfield farmhouse and go through the white squeeze stile and down the farm drive. Turn left at the road and enter Beaminster outskirts. Just before reaching the B road look out for the gate on your right leading into a paddock. Follow this path back to the church and the square.

Mapperton Gardens, Beaminster
Several acres of terraced hillside gardens surround a manor house dating back to the 16th century. Fountains, grottoes, stone fishponds, an orangery, good views and walks. Courtyard Fair in Sep. Open daily Mar to Oct. Telephone: 0308 862645.

Horn Park Garden
(north of Beaminster)
Formal gardens include a wild-flower meadow, woodland walks and panoramic views out to sea. Open Apr to Oct. Telephone: 0308 862212.

ℋIGHER BOCKHAMPTON ~to~ 𝒲EST STAFFORD

APPROXIMATELY 6 MILES

A gentle, varied and peaceful walk through woodland, water-meadows and pasture and across heathland in an area much loved by the author Thomas Hardy.

Parking

OS Map 194 SY7292. Free car park close to Thomas Hardy's cottage, signposted off A35.

Wise Man Inn

West Stafford, Dorchester. Three miles east of Dorchester, off A352.

FURTHER EXPLORATION

Thomas Hardy's Cottage

The novelist was born here in 1840 and this was his childhood home. The interior can be viewed by appointment only from Apr to Oct. Telephone: 0305 262366.

St Michael's Church, Stinsford

Thomas Hardy was baptised at St Michael's in July 1840 . His heart was buried here in his

From Hardy's Cottage leave on the footpath to Rushy Pond, keeping left with a yellow arrow after 100yds. At Rushy Pond take the path signed Norris Hill, following yellow markers on trees and posts through the wood and over open heathland to a stile. Turn right, climb another stile into a meadow, then follow the left-hand fence towards a house. Cross the lane onto a farm track, keeping left of the barns, then bear right (blue arrow) and after quarter of a mile cross a river. Join the gated track ahead, shortly to take the right fork at four gates and continue along a grassy track to a further gate (yellow arrow) and cross a footbridge. Bear left to the stile and then a gate, cross the river and pass Lewell Mill to a road. Turn right onto a footpath (yellow arrow) then at a stile cross a field to a stile in the hedge opposite. Continue over the next field, through a gap in the hedge, then bear slightly left to a stile (cottages on left). Cross and head diagonally left uphill (past an electricity pole) towards trees and roofs on the skyline. On reaching the road turn right for West Stafford and the pub.

Wise Man Inn *(Devenish)*

This historic thatched pub faces the tiny village school. Formerly the school mistress's house, it takes its name from Wiseman Cottage round the corner, which was the original village alehouse. The traditional interior boasts collections of toby jugs and old pipes. Children are welcome in the lounge and there is a garden.

On draught: Royal Wessex Bitter, Boddingtons Bitter, Guinness, Murphy's.
Food: there are specials like lamb madras (£3.95), chicken tikka (£4.95) and steak and kidney pie (£4.75) and popular snacks like filled jacket potatoes (from £1.75), macaroni cheese (£3.50), ham, egg and chips (£3.50) and five different ploughman's (from £3.25).

Times: 12-2pm and 7-9pm (except Sun evenings in winter). Telephone: 0305 263694.

From the pub turn right along the road past the church and over the river. Immediately, turn left through a gate to take the river path, then round the meadow edge to a squeeze stile in the corner. Head across the field towards a white house, climb the stile onto the track and turn right to the road. Turn left, then right along the bridleway to Dorchester. Continue along the road, pass under the flyover, then turn right onto the track signed Stinsford. Cross the river, turn right (back under flyover), shortly to climb the stile at the end of the track onto a path across a watermeadow and over the stream. At a signpost turn left (Grey Bridge), then right, signed Stinsford. Pass the church, walk up the lane past a farm, right, and down to a crossroads. Turn right, then beyond Birkin House take the path left, signed Higher Bockhampton, running parallel to the road. At the bridleway turn left then diagonally right up the field for Higher Bockhampton. At the farm follow the track out to the road, turn left, then right for the car park.

first wife's grave in 1928, his ashes being interred in Westminster Abbey. An interesting booklet giving details of 'Hardy Connections' in the area is available in the church.

Dorchester

The county town of Dorset has some interesting places to visit, such as the County Museum, the Military Museum, a Dinosaur Museum and the Tutankhamun Exhibition. For further information telephone: 0305 267992

Maiden Castle
(1m south-west of Dorchester)

An Iron-Age fort that ranks among the finest in Britain covering 47 acres. Accessible at any reasonable time. Splendid views.

ᴍINTERNE MAGNA
~to~ ℰERNE ABBAS

**APPROXIMATELY
5 MILES**

❖◆❖

*A demanding walk,
rewarded by superb
views along the Cerne
Valley and passing
the Cerne Giant
carved in the chalk
hillside.*

❖◆❖

Start of walk
OS Map 194 Ref SY6504.
By Minterne Magna Church

ᴛake the bridleway beside the church, signposted Buckland Newton. After Keepers Cottage proceed uphill to where the track bears right, then fork left (yellow arrow) through a gate and head on up via a series of gates to the ridge. Turn right onto a stony track and after quarter of a mile take the track to the right and head downhill. Turn left at a crossroads of tracks just before Minterne Parva, back towards the hill. Where the main track turns right carry straight on uphill (hedge on right) to a gate. Turn right and continue up via a series of gates to a crossroads of tracks at the top. Turn right, pass an open-frame barn and head across the field to a stile to the right of a clump of trees. Cross, bear left and continue through the remains of a settlement and along the ridge. With Cerne Abbas in view make for the left side of the fenced-off enclosure, then follow the steep path downhill, cross a stile and go through the arched gateway into the graveyard, out along Church St, right at the main street and the pub is on the left.

New Inn *(Eldridge Pope)*

A former coaching inn built in the mid-16th century, with mullioned windows, a stone roof and a cobbled courtyard. A single large bar has a woodburner, tapestry-covered wall benches and old farming implements, traps and harnesses adorning the walls. At the back is a beer garden. Children are welcome in the dining area. Guest bedrooms are available.

On draught: Eldridge Pope Dorchester Bitter, Hardy Country Ale, Royal Oak, Guinness, good selection of wines by the glass.

Food: an extensive menu ranges from a help-yourself salad bar to daily home-made dishes like spinach, goat's cheese and walnut pancakes (£4.50), leek and Stilton pie (£4.95), fisherman's bake (£6.50) and braised leg of guinea fowl with orange sauce (£6.75). Also available are ploughman's (£3.50) and double-decker toasted sandwiches (£3.75). Puddings (£3.00) include chocolate roulade and strawberry nut meringue.

Times: 12-2pm and 6-9.30pm. Telephone: 0300 341274.

---

ross the road and walk along Duck Street until you reach 'Giant Viewpoint' and the A352. Carry on along the verge for 200 yards, then cross and proceed to the minor road, signposted Upcerne. Follow the lane for quarter of a mile, then where the lane bears left, take the footpath straight ahead through a pair of white gates. Cross a lane onto the footpath opposite which soon drops down to another lane. Turn left, then shortly turn right up the bridleway lined with sycamores. At the top bear left, then immediately seek a gap in the hedge on the right to a gate (blue arrow). Follow the right-hand edge of the field to the gate visible below, diagonally left. Continue diagonally downhill to the far corner of the meadow, then turn right through the gate and follow the avenue of elms to the main road. Go left for the village and car park.

New Inn
14 Long Street, Cerne Abbas - village centre.

FURTHER EXPLORATION

Cerne Abbas
The village derives its name from a Benedictine abbey founded in AD 987. Monastic remains include a beautiful 15th-century gatehouse, a 14th-century guesthouse and a 15th-century tithe barn that has been converted into a home. Early examples of heraldic stained glass can be seen in the windows of the church.

Cerne Abbas Giant
No one knows the origin of the figure of the great naked giant carved in the hillside overlooking the village. It is believed to be associated with fertility rites and may predate the Roman occupation.

Minterne Gardens, Minterne Magna
Lakes, cascades, streams and many fine and rare trees are found in these splendid landscaped gardens. The present mansion (not open) dates from the Edwardian period. Garden open daily Apr to Oct. Telephone: 0300 341370.

$\mathcal{A}$VINGTON ~to~ $\mathcal{O}$VINGTON

APPROXIMATELY 6 MILES

A tranquil ramble through the delightful Itchen Valley along riverside, field and woodland paths and quiet lanes. Look out for herons, kingfishers and the trout swimming in the crystal clear chalk stream.

Start of walk
OS Map 185 Ref SU5232. Car park and picnic area near the lake at Avington Park.

Bush Inn
Ovington, Alresford. Village signposted off the A31 between Alresford and Winchester.

**FURTHER EXPLORATION
Alresford**
One of Hampshire's most picturesque small towns with its wide Broad Street lined with Georgian houses, speciality shops and pubs. In medieval days, Alresford was an important wool town. Broad Street leads down to a medieval causeway (now a road) that was built to create Alresford Pond - an important refuge for wildfowl.

From the car park turn left along the lane, crossing a cattle grid, then at a T-junction turn left downhill through Avington. Where the road bears left keep ahead, shortly to take the waymarked track right. Follow the track uphill, then left behind trees, go across a farm track and follow the arrowed path along the field edge and through a clump of trees, soon to bear left along a hedge to a stile. Keep left downhill to a further stile and lane. Turn right (Itchen Way), then left along the drive to Yavington Farm, keeping to the right of the house to a stile in the hedge. Proceed ahead to another stile, then keep left-handed round the field edge to a stile and turn left to cross two footbridges over the River Itchen. Cross a meadow to a stile beside a gate, follow the track beside cottages to the B-road and turn right into Itchen Stoke. Shortly, turn right down Water Lane, cross a small footbridge at the bottom, bear left along the riverside path and in quarter of a mile cross over the river for the pub.

⇔*Bush Inn* (Free House)⇔

This fine old rose-covered pub stands idyllically beside the gently flowing River Itchen and is a delightful spot for summer drinking. Inside, the charming dimly-lit bars have open fires, bottle-green walls, large rustic scrubbed pine tables, high-backed settles and old wooden chairs. Various copper pans and old hunting prints adorn the walls. Children are welcome at lunchtime in the bottom bar.

On draught: Gales HSB, Wadworth 6X, Flowers Original, Hall and Woodhouse Tanglefoot, guest ale, Guinness, Stella Artois, fine choice of country wines by the glass.
Food: home-cooked food includes a daily-changing specials board which may feature soup (£1.95), chicken and ham pasta with garlic bread and salad (£5.95),

chilli con carne (£5.50), grilled Itchen trout (£6.50) and scallops in a ginger and coriander sauce served on a bed of tagliatelle (£7.25). **Times:** 12-2pm and 6.30-9.45pm (Sun 7-9pm). Restaurant meals 7.30-9.30pm only. Telephone: 0962 732764.

---

*L*eave the pub, turn right uphill into Ovington and take the first lane right at the telephone box, signed Easton. Beyond Lovington Cottages and the entrance to Lovington House, drop downhill, shortly to take the waymarked hedged path on your left. Gradually ascend into woodland (Hampage Wood), remaining on the path to a junction of paths in front of Hampage Farm. Turn right and follow a broad track through the wood, leaving it via a gate and soon reach Avington Manor Farm and a lane. Turn right and stay on this quiet lane back into Avington, turning left to rejoin your outward route back to the car park.

Mid-Hants Railway,
Alresford
Also known as the Watercress Line, because it was once the major despatch point for watercress, the track has been restored and is run by enthusiasts between Alton and Alresford. Steam trains run regularly during the summer and on December weekends, visiting four stations on the journey.

River Itchen
One of the finest unspoilt chalk streams in Europe, with a naturally breeding population of brown and rainbow trout. It also supports a good birdlife, namely grebes, duck, herons and species of warbler.

$\mathcal{E}$MPSHOTT ~to~ $\mathcal{H}$AWKLEY

**APPROXIMATELY
4½ MILES**

*A peaceful rural
ramble exploring a
section of the Hangers
Way and established
old paths and tracks
around the
Rother Valley.*

Start of walk
OS Map 186 Ref SU7531.
By the lane at Empshott
church.

Hawkley Inn Hawkley, Liss.
Two miles off A325 at West
Liss.

FURTHER EXPLORATION

**Gilbert White's House
and the Oates
Exhibition,** Selborne
This historic house, with its
glorious garden, was the
home of the famous 18th-
century naturalist and curate of
Selborne, Gilbert White, author
of 'The Natural History of
Selborne'. Displays include an
exhibition on the Captain
Oates who accompanied Scott
to the South Pole and Frank
Oates, a Victorian explorer and
naturalist in America and
Africa.

*F*rom the church, head left along the lane to the T-junction, turn left steeply downhill and take the waymarked path right across a stile beside a gate. Keep left uphill through scrub to a stile, then keep right-handed along a paddock fence. Step through the fence keep left through a gate and follow the gravel driveway beside a house to a lane. Turn right remaining on the lane to cross a ford. Bear off left to a stile, then follow the defined path across a field to a stile and along the right-hand edge of the field beyond to a lane. Turn left, then just beyond Vann Farm and a pond cross a stile on the right (Hangers Way), and keep right-handed along the edge of two fields towards the wooded ridge ahead. Cross a couple of stiles and join the well-worn path through the woodland fringe at the base of the ridge, ignoring two paths on the left. After three-quarters of a mile, level with Hawkley, and where the path bears right with the woodland, turn left to follow a field path, shortly passing houses to reach a lane. Turn left into Hawkley and keep right at the green for the pub.

$\backsim$*Hawkley Inn* (Free House)$\backsim$

This homely village inn with a tiled façade and covered front verandah has a main bar and a tiny, adjacent no-smoking room, furnished with old leather armchairs, church pews and pine tables. There is also a restaurant Walkers and cyclists are warmly welcomed, as are children and at weekends this friendly inn is a popular destination.

On draught: Ballard's Trotton Ale and Best Bitter, Ringwood Fortyniner and Porter, Arkells 3B, Guinness, Stella Artois.
Food: hearty snacks may include lettuce and bacon or watercress soup (£2.50), pork liver pâté and toast (£2), beef and mushroom casserole (£4.95), lasagne (£4.75) filled jacket potatoes (from £2.75) and filled rolls (from

£1.60). Puddings include chocolate roulade and bread and butter pudding.

Times: 12-2pm and 7-9.30 pm, except Sun evening.
Telephone: 0730 84205.

White's grave is in the churchyard and much of the countryside around Selborne is owned by the National Trust. Open Mar to Oct and weekends Nov and Dec. Telephone: 042050 275.

●━━◆━━●

*T*urn left on leaving the pub, then at a T-junction of lanes, proceed straight across to follow a waymarked fenced path to another lane. Turn left, head downhill past Uplands on your right, then at a left-hand bend take the arrowed path right. Shortly, climb a stile, then bear diagonally left across pasture to a gate and drop down onto an established trackway. Turn right and shortly pass an old timbered cottage on your left, then take the centre one of three tracks, leading between outbuildings/workshops and gradually descending beside woodland to a gate. Continue straight ahead through pasture, keeping left of a metal trough and a track to the right, to a gate and cross a bridge over the River Rother. Climb up a stony track to a lane, turn left and follow it back to Empshott church.

*K*EYHAVEN ~to~ *P*ENNINGTON

APPROXIMATELY 4½ MILES

A level, easy going coastal walk along the Solent Way, returning across open fields and gravel tracks. Good views across the Solent to the Isle of Wight.

Parking
OS Map 196 Ref SU3091. Car park (charge) in the centre of Keyhaven village.

*F*rom the car park turn right along the adjacen road, go over the bridge and soon turn right alon a waymarked path around the perimeter of Keyhaver Harbour. Keep to the defined path along the length o the shoreline (Solent Way) past Pennington Marshe and historic salt beds. Beyond a wooden gate, near jetty, follow the gravel track inland and pass throug two more gates to a lane. Turn right, then take th arrowed path right just beyond a sharp left-hand bend following it past several houses and Oxey Farm to gate and a lane. Follow the lane round to Chequer Green and the pub.

Chequers Inn (Whitbread)

Tucked away along a lane this 400-year-old unspoil inn was once the local salt exchange, marketing sal yielded from the nearby tidal marshes. The low beamed interior is full of character, with various ol

ables, wall pews and country-style chairs on a part-
iled and boarded floor. For winter cosiness there is a
voodburning stove and for the warmer months, the
nn's delightful courtyard acts as a suntrap and there is
lso a sheltered garden where you can enjoy a peaceful
Irink in relaxing surroundings. Children are welcome
nside as long as they are away from the bar.

In draught: Flowers Original, Wadworth 6X,
Vhitbread Strong Country Ale, guest ales, Heineken,
•tella Artois, good choice of wines.

"ood: the regularly changing blackboard menu
eatures good, home-cooked dishes and may list split
•ea and ham soup (£1.95), moules marinière (£3.75),
Mediterranean fish soup (£3.50), avocado and pasta
ake (£5.20), rack of lamb with a honey and lime glaze
£7.95) and char-grilled rump steak (£9.50). There is
xcellent fish, such as baked sea bream with mixed
erbs (£6.95). Puddings (£2). The restaurant has its own
eparate menu.

"imes: 12-2pm and 7-10pm. Telephone: 0590 673415.

---

*L*eave the inn, turn right and immediately right
again along a private lane, (which is also a
•aymarked footpath). Keep right just before the
ntrance to Pennington House to cross a stile and
•llow the path beside a house to another stile and a
.eld. Keep right beside the hedge, shortly to pass
hrough it into the next field. Turn left and proceed
long the field edge to a stile and cross into a lane.
urn left, then soon turn right onto an arrowed path
hrough a metal gate. Shortly, cross a stile and follow a
rack beside a lake to reach a stile leading onto a road -
ou will see a refuse tip entrance to your left. Cross this
•ad and another stile onto a gravel track, bear left and
•llow this long and winding path between fields and
uarries to a stile beside a gate. Cross over and turn
ght along the lane, following it back into Keyhaven
nd so to the car park.

Chequers Inn
Ridgeway Lane, Pennington,
Lymington. South off A337 at
roundabout in Pennington,
west of Lymington.

FURTHER EXPLORATION

Hurst Castle, near Keyhaven
The castle is one of the many
coastal forts built by Henry VIII
in case of invasion, and was
occupied in the Civil War and
then fortified again in the 19th
century. It has good views to
the Isle of Wight and can be
reached on foot or by a
summer ferry from Keyhaven.
Open daily (except Mon in
winter) all year. Telephone:
0590 642344.

Pennington Marshes
Once this area was important
in the salt industry until its
decline in the mid 19th
century. Today the marshes are
a refuge for wildlife, especially
for a large number of nesting
birds during the summer,
including terns.

𝒟EVIZES ~to~ 𝑅OWDE

APPROXIMATELY 6 MILES

An easy walk mainly along the Kennet and Avon Canal, including the spectacular flight of locks which climbs 234ft in less than two miles.

From the car park cross the canal by way of the stone bridge behind the Visitor Centre and turn left along the towpath, signposted to Caen Hill Locks. At the next road cross the canal and continue on the left bank for nearly two miles down past the flight of locks. At the bottom of the flight, go under a road bridge and proceed past five more locks to a footbridge just beyond. Cross and double back (right) for several hundred yards, then follow an arrow on your left to a stile and take the path through the meadow (keeping the hedge on your left). Climb the next stile, bear right along a hedged path which soon becomes a track, then at a T-junction turn left (opposite a ruined barn) and shortly right down Rowde Court Road. After 200yds you will come to a footpath on the left which takes you through the churchyard and emerges on the main road near the pub.

George and Dragon (Wadworth)

Set well above the A432 the plain unassuming exterior hides an attractive and welcoming bar dating back to the 17th century. Wooden floorboards, panelling, beams and a assortment of old country tables, farmhouse chairs and solid benches create a unspoilt atmosphere. A carved stone fireplace with a good open fire warms the bar when the weather is cold. Children are welcome in the pub as long as they are away from the bar.

On draught: Wadworth IPA and 6X, Guinness, Heineken, Kronenbourg.

Food: daily-changing blackboard menus list the extensive range of inventive and sometimes unusual dishes on offer, such as Provençale fish soup (£4.50), tagliatelle pesto (£4.50), garlic fish pâté (£4), salmon fishcakes with Hollandaise (£4 or £7), gratin of chicken savoyarde (£6), ploughman's with home-made pickles (£4.50). The menu can usuallly offer at least eight fresh-fish dishes, featuring, for example, fillet of turbot with crab sauce (£12) and barracuda with mussel sauce (£11). Puddings (£3) include gooseberry crumble and blackberry meringue pie.

Times: 12-2pm and 7-10pm (except Sun evening and all day Mon).Telephone: 0380 723053.

———————◆◆◆———————

From the pub turn right along the main road, then right again (signposted Marsh Lane, Poulshot) by the Cross Keys public house and follow the pavement to the end of the village. Continue along the road, until you come to a right-hand bend. After this, take the track on your left heading towards Caen Hill Locks and waymarked Prison Bridge. Rejoin the canal and follow the left bank this time (bearing left on a track round the Waterways compound), When you eventually reach a road, cross to the opposite bank of the canal and retrace your outward route to get back to the Canal Centre car park.

Parking
OS Map 173 Ref SU0061.
Pay and display car park at the Canal Centre, north of Devizes town centre.

George and Dragon
Rowde, Devizes. On A342 Devizes to Chippenham road.

FURTHER EXPLORATION

Kennet and Avon Canal Visitor Centre, Devizes
Housed in a former granary built to serve the canal, the Centre explains the construction and history of the canal, which was opened on 28th December 1810 to link Bristol with Reading. There are 29 locks in the famous flight outside town, with 16 of them rising like steps up Caen Hill. Telephone: 0380 721279.

Wadworth Brewery, Devizes
Tours of the brewery, which was built in 1885 on the old Northgate side of town and still runs horse-drawn drays, can be arranged. Telephone: 0380 723361.

Oliver's Castle
(2½ miles north of Devizes)
A remarkable hill, topped by an ancient fort, with good views, excellent picnic site and nature trail.

CASTLE COMBE ~to~ FORD

An undulating though not too strenuous walk exploring leafy river valleys, returning via the Bybrook Valley and the centre of Castle Combe, one of England's most picturesque villages.

Parking:
OS Map 173 Ref ST8477. Free car park north of Castle Combe, just south of B4039.

Turn right out of the car park, then right again at the T-junction, shortly to take the footpath right signposted Nettleton Shrub. At the end of the tarmac drive cross the stile and bear left around the golf course keeping to the footpath (blue posts). Follow the path down through trees and cross a river, the posts shortly directing you off the golf course into woods. On reaching some buildings turn right through a kissing gate under an archway, then go left between the buildings and follow the river bank path. Cross a stile beside a metal gate, turn left over the slab bridge across the river and proceed up the steep and stony path to a track, then a road. Turn left, pass Shrub Farm then at a road junction take the footpath right signposted Ford. Go through woods, over a stile and above a valley, then look out for a post marking a path steeply downhill to cross a stream. Proceed through a meadow, then up steps in an earth bank and continue through the trees to the outskirts of Ford. At the main road turn right, then take the next left to the pub.

❧ *White Hart (Free House)* ❧

Nestling beside the River Bybrook, this mellow stone 16th-century inn is full of charm and character. Heavy beams, dark half-panelled walls, old settles and rustic tables and chairs are features of the oldest part of the pub, the main bar, which has the date 1553 carved into the lintel above its ancient fireplace. There are two dining areas, where children are welcome, furnished with some antique pieces and decorated with prints and plates. For warmer weather there is a riverside terrace. Attractive guest bedrooms are available, some in the converted stable block across the lane.

On draught: Hall and Woodhouse Badger Bitter and Tanglefoot, Wadworth 6X, Bass, Marston's Pedigree, Flowers IPA, Smiles Exhibition, five guest ales, Guinness, Stella Artois, Dry Blackthorn cider.

Food: daily-changing lunchtime fare may include spinach soup (£1.50), moussaka (£4.50), ploughman's (from £3.50), hot filled baguettes (£2.95), and grilled fillet of cod with herb butter (£4.25). Evening choices are more imaginative, such as breast of chicken with oven-roasted baby vegetables and garlic cream sauce (£6.95) and fillet of mullet with a light salad of frisée leaves and orange segments on a citrus sauce (£9.95). **Times**: 12-2pm and 7-9pm. Telephone: 0249 782213.

From the pub go back to the main road and turn right, then shortly take the road left, signposted Castle Combe. Proceed uphill and at the edge of woodland cross a stile on the right and follow the path down to Long Dean. Cross the river bridge, taking the next lane left past Rose Cottage. This soon becomes a track, then beyond a stepped stile, on top of Rack Hill, gradually descend for ¾ mile on a path through woodland to more open ground and shortly cross the river. Turn right on the road into Castle Combe. At the market cross, keep right, uphill back to the car park.

White Hart
Ford, Chippenham. Off A420 between Chippenham and Bristol.

FURTHER EXPLORATION
Castle Combe
Lying deep in a stream-threaded combe, this is acknowledged as one of England's most picturesque villages. The 13th--century market cross and numerous old houses are interesting and the riches of the wool trade contributed to the building of St Andrew's Church, which has some fine stone carvings, and a chancel dating back to 1250. The village was transformed into a harbour (by damming the stream) for a scene in the film of Dr Doolittle.

Sheldon Manor
(3 miles east of Ford)
A Plantagenet manor house with a 13th-century porch and a 15th-century chapel set in beautiful gardens. Telephone: 0249 653120.

Corsham Court
(4 miles south east of Ford)
This fine Elizabethan manor built in 1582 houses a fascinating collection of paintings, statues and furniture. It is set in gardens and parkland designed by Capability Brown with a 13-acre lake. Telephone: 0249 712214.

OLD SARUM
~to~ LOWER WOODFORD

APPROXIMATELY 6 MILES

An undulating chalk downland walk affording views of Old Sarum and the distant spire of Salisbury cathedral, returning along the delightful Woodford Valley.

Parking
OS Map 184 Ref SU1332. Free car park at Old Sarum Castle, off A35 north of Salisbury. Open as castle; gates locked 6pm in summer, 4pm in winter.

Wheatsheaf Inn
Lower Woodford, Salisbury - off A36 north of Salisbury.

FURTHER EXPLORATION
Old Sarum
The history of this huge Iron Age camp spans 5,000 years. It was an important town and cathedral complex in Norman times and when the new cathedral was built in New Sarum, or Salisbury, the community was gradually abandoned. Plays and tournaments are held here in the summer. Open daily 10am-6pm in summer, 10am-4pm in winter. Telephone: 0722 335398.

ollow the car park drive back to a right-hand bend, then ignore the stile and gated track on the left and go through the adjacent two smaller wooden gates onto a footpath. Shortly cross a lane and continue on the track over the hill into the next valley, maintaining direction past a thatched cottage. The track becomes stony, then grassy as it climbs uphill. As you pass under the electricity cables, take the narrow footpath amongst the trees to reach a gate. Do not go through, but turn left along the bridleway down to Salterton Farm. Turn left at the road, then shortly right down a No Through lane to cross the River Avon and emerge on the village street. Bear left for the pub.

Wheatsheaf Inn *(Hall and Woodhouse)*

An attractive, 18th-century, creeper-clad inn, the Wheatsheaf is set in the picturesque Woodford Valley, close to the River Avon. The rambling bar consists of a series of inter-connecting rooms with some unusual carved seats and other sturdy tables and chairs. Brick fireplace, indoor fishpond, horsebrasses and plates make an attractive and welcoming atmosphere. The snug Cabin Bar has a large inglenook, barrel seats and games. Children are welcome in the dining room and there is a large walled garden with play area.

On draught: Hall and Woodhouse Badger Best, Tanglefoot and Hard Tackle, Guinness, Hofbrau lagers.
Food: a wide choice of home-made dishes may include lentil and carrot soup (£1.40), open sandwiches (from £3.15), ploughman's (from £3.05), chicken and mushroom pie (£4.95), salmon steak (£5.35), lamb rogan josh (£4.75), chilli (£3.95), steaks (from £7.95) and a selection of nine vegetarian dishes (from £2.60). Desserts range from spotted dick (£2.25) to profiteroles (£2.30).
Times: 12-2 pm and 7-10 pm. Telephone 0722 73203

From the pub turn right and follow the road for half a mile. Turn left onto a waymarked track, then at The Bays go through a farm gate on your left and continue with the hedge on your right. At the field's edge cross a stile and follow the arrow left to another stile and bridge, then bear right along the stream's edge to a stone bridge. Turn right onto the drive, then left at the main road. In half a mile, take the track right past Avon Farm as far as a stile on your left. Cross this and maintain direction ahead with the river to the left, until you reach a tarmac path, then turn left across the river. Follow the path to the road and turn right along the pavement, crossing over and turning left beside Dairy Cottage, up the bridleway signposted Old Sarum. Fork right over a stile and continue (with the hedge on your left) anti-clockwise around the grassy rampart back to the car park.

Heale House Garden,
Middle Woodford
Eight acres of beautiful garden bordering the River Avon surround a fine 17th-century manor house (tours by arrangement). Features are a rose garden, authentic Japanese Tea House, and a plant centre. Open daily all year. Telephone: 0722 73504.

Stonehenge
(north of Woodford Valley)
England's most famous prehistoric monument dates back 5000 years. Originally comprising an encircling ditch and bank from the Stone Age period, it developed into circles of sarsen stones around a horseshoe of trilithons enclosing the enigmatic Welsh bluestones. Several stones weighing over 50 tons still stand. Open daily all year. Telephone: 0722 734472.

OLD HEATHFIELD ~to~ WARBLETON

**APPROXIMATELY
4 MILES**

*An undulating
farmland ramble with
good views of the
South Downs.*

Start of Walk
OS Map 199 Ref TQ5920.
On School Hill, outside cricket
ground in Old Heathfield.

War-Bill-in-Tun Inn
Warbleton, near Heathfield.
Village signposted off B2096 at
Punnetts Town, east of
Heathfield.

Walk downhill, bearing off left to enter the churchyard, then bear left round the church to a lane. Keep left, then before Highlands Cottage, bear right to a stile and follow a grassy path to a drive and kissing gate. Bear half-left to a stile in the corner, then follow the left-hand field edge to a stile and cross the lane. Pass through a gate onto a narrow path downhill, skirting an old lake and marshy area to a stile. Bear left, keep ahead across pasture towards a house to a gate and a track. Turn left, pass beside a garage to a stile by a gate (yellow arrow), then keep right-handed to a stile and crossroads of paths. Keep straight on, bearing right shortly to follow a muddy path through trees and over another crossroads of paths to a stile. Bear diagonally right across pasture, pass through a gap in the hedge, then bear half-left to pass between a telegraph pole and pond to enter woodland via a stile. Leave the wood, cross pasture to a stile to the right of a green-roofed barn, then make for a stile in the right-hand field corner and follow arrowed path to a lane. Turn left, then right onto the drive to Boring House Farm,

immediately bearing half-right across pasture to a stile on the edge of a copse. Keep left through fields downhill to a footbridge, then climb a worn path to a stile. Keep right-handed to another stile, maintaining course on a defined path to Warbleton church. Before reaching the lane, turn right through the churchyard to the pub.

❧ *War-Bill-in-Tun Inn (Free House)* ❧

An attractive and peaceful 15th-century village inn about which many stories are told: tales of contraband, priest holes and ghosts. The modernised low-beamed bar has comfortable seating and features a huge inglenook fireplace. Both dogs and children are welcome in the bar.

On draught: Courage Directors, Harveys Best Bitter, guest ale, Guinness, Heineken.
Food: a good range of dishes includes soup (£1.40), ploughman's (£2.95), sandwiches (from £1.45), steak and kidney pie (£4.55), beef curry (£4.50), seafood platter (£5.65), Gressingham duck (£10.15) and fillet steak (£11.25). There are specials like lasagne (£4.75) and guinea fowl (£7.95) and a vegetarian menu. Puddings range from chocolate and rum gateau to steamed syrup pudding.
Times: 12-1.45pm, 7-9.30pm. Telephone: 0435 830636.

*R*eturn through the churchyard, then bear half-left across a large field, pass through the hedge onto a lane, just left of a cottage. Turn left and go downhill, cross a small stream, then at a crossroads of tracks (barn to left), turn right uphill along a stony track. Keep left of a house, the track becoming grassy as it runs parallel with woodland and shortly pass through a field entrance by an oak tree, before descending to cross a small brook. Pass through a gate, climb a stile on the right, then keep left-handed to a further stile in the corner. Turn right, follow the field edge and grounds of Heathfield House, via gates, to the kissing gate on the outward route and so back to your car.

FURTHER EXPLORATION

Warbleton
In 1557 Richard Woodman, the local ironmaster and church warden, was burnt at the stake in Lewes for having called his rector 'Mr Facing-Both-Ways' for being a Protestant under Henry VIII and a Catholic under Mary. His story is told on the west wall of the nave in the church. Woodman is said to have sought refuge in the inn whilst on the run. Legend has it that the unusual pub name originated during the Civil War when marauding soldiers, intent on getting a drink, tapped a barrel of beer with a battle axe - War-Bill-in-Tun.

Bateman's, Burwash
Rudyard Kipling lived at this fine 17th-century ironmaster's house from 1902 to 1936. His study and room are left as they were in his day. Beautiful gardens. (National Trust) Open Apr to Oct. Telephone: 0435 882302.

Michelham Priory, Upper Dicker, Hailsham
The Augustinian priory dates from 1229, and there are also a 14th-century gatehouse and a 16th-century house with interesting furniture, tapestries and stained glass. The six acres of gardens feature a watermill, a ropemaking museum and a programme of special events. Telephone: 0323 844224.

$\mathcal{S}$OUTHWATER ~to~ $\mathcal{N}$UTHURST

**APPROXIMATELY
5 MILES**

*A peaceful,
waymarked ramble
through farmland
across field paths and
established bridleways*

Parking
OS Map 198 Ref TQ1525.
Southwater Country Park,
Cripplegate Lane, signposted
off A24.

Turn left on leaving the park's main entrance and right along Strakers Lane, waymarked Downs Link walk. Pass beneath A24, then where the lane bears left, proceed straight ahead to follow a narrow path along a fence to a footbridge and stile beyond. Bear half-left across pasture to two stiles, keep left to cross another stile, then pass between paddocks to a stile and lane. Turn right, then left at the T-junction and shortly right (blue arrow) to follow a path left-handed through pasture into woodland via a gate. On emerging from the trees, keep left along the woodland edge to a stile, then cross pasture to a small gate and keep ahead on a drive between stables and a house. At a junction of paths, keep on between paddocks, cross a gallop and soon a concrete bridge over a stream to a gate. Keep left-handed round the field edge on a path through two belts of trees via gates, then along the left-hand edge of pasture to a lane. Turn left to the pub.

☙Black Horse *(Free House)*☙

On its quiet village lane, this attractive 17th-century brick cottage is a delightful walking destination. The unspoilt, heavily beamed bars are traditionally furnished, there is a huge log fire and old photographs adorn the walls. There is a splendid secluded garden and terrace outside. Children are very welcome inside.

On draught: Harveys Sussex Bitter, Tetley, Wadworth 6X, Adnams Bitter, Greene King Abbot Ale, Guinness.
Food: the hearty daily specials may be beef stroganoff (£6.50), lamb and rosemary pie (£5.50), or sweet and sour pork (£6.50). Regular dishes may include chicken curry (£5.95), fisherman's pie (£6.50), sandwiches and ploughman's. Puddings (£2.25) include treacle and nut tart. Summer weekends bring regular barbecues.
Times: 11am-2.30pm, 6-10pm. Sun 12-3pm, 7-10.30pm.
Telephone 0403 891272.

*C*ross the lane on leaving the pub, to follow a waymarked path along the metalled drive to Nuthurst Farm. Proceed round the farm on a gravel track, keeping ahead to where it bears right to a bungalow, then at a T-junction of waymarked tracks, turn left, shortly to bear off right where the path curves left towards a house. A finger post directs you along a bridleway which becomes hedged, than at a crossroads of signposted paths, turn right to follow an established earth track. Keep ahead at the next finger post, then on nearing the farm, bear off left with a waymarker across rough pasture to a stile, cross a footbridge, then follow a narrow path to a stile. Keep ahead over pasture to cross a lane via two stiles, then bear half-left to a gate where you turn right through two more gates before crossing pasture to a stile and lane opposite Lockyers Farm. Turn left, then shortly right onto a waymarked path through a metal gate and along the right-hand edge of two fields, crossing a small bridge to a gate. Join a wide track, pass round Strakers Farm and follow the drive beside A24 to rejoin your outward route to the Country Park.

Black Horse
Nuthurst Street, Nuthurst, Horsham. Village signposted off A281 south-east of Horsham.

FURTHER EXPLORATION

Southwater Country Park
One of Britain's youngest Country Parks providing an interesting example of transformation from a former industrial site into a recreational and wildlife reserve covering 54 acres. Visitor Centre.

Leonardslee Gardens, Lower Beeding
This splendid landscaped garden on the edge of St Leonard's Forest comprises 200 acres of grounds that are open to the public. They are best seen at two different seasons - in the spring for azaleas and rhododendrons and in the autumn for the amazing foliage colours. There are also a rock garden, a Japanese garden, a Bonsai exhibition and a garden centre. Open Apr to Oct. Telephone 0403 891212.

ƒITTLEWORTH ~to~ ßYWORTH

APPROXIMATELY 6 MILES

An enjoyable and interesting walk across common and farmland, affording splendid views of the South Downs

Parking:
OS Map 197 Ref TQ0019. Parking area at Hewsworth Common, west of Fittleworth at the junction of B2138 and A283.

From the car park follow the waymarked path straight ahead onto the common to a junction of five footpaths. Turn right down some steps, following a sandy path across a junction of paths and to a lane. Turn left, bear right and take signed path right, beside Rew Cottage. Keep right-handed through two fields, cross a brook, then a stile in fencing left and turn right to a gate. Keep left on a track past a house, then at a T-junction of tracks, turn right and eventually turn right onto a lane beyond a pair of cottages. Shortly, bear off left with fingerpost to a stile, then keep right-handed through pasture to a stile. Turn left to a stile and join a track between cottages and a barn. Soon turn right onto a grassy trackway between fields (fingerpost obscured) and proceed to a stile near a house. Bear left along driveway, then cross the waymarked stile on the right and head diagonally right to a stile and B-road. Cross over, turn right, ignore fingerpost left and cross the brook and stile left. Keep left of the hedge to a stile, pass through a scrub area beside the brook to a stile, then proceed ahead to a fingerpost and junction of paths. Turn right uphill to a stile, follow the narrow path to a drive and lane, then turn left for a quarter of a mile to the pub.

⊷Black Horse⊷
(Free House)

This unusual three-storey pub with a Georgian façade hides an ancient interior dating back to the 14th century. Wooden floors, half-panelled walls, open fires and an

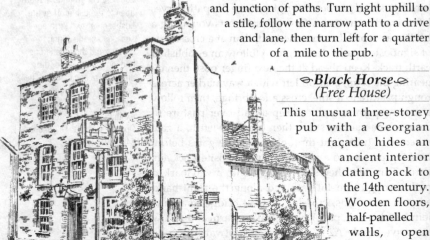

assortment of rustic chairs and scrubbed tables characterise the three inter-connecting rooms. Super terraced garden with valley views. Children welcome in eating area.

On draught: Youngs Best Bitter and Special, Ballards Wassail, Harveys Sussex Bitter, Eldridge Pope Hardy Country Ale, Guinness, Lowenbrau, Carlsberg, Dry Blackthorn cider. **Food:** an interesting range of bar food may include sardines in garlic (£3.95), vegetable casserole au gratin (£5.50), oriental chicken (£7.50), ham, egg and chips (£4.95), ploughman's (from £3.50) and daily specials like steak, Guinness and oyster pie (£6.95). Sunday roasts (£5.95)

Times: 11.30am-1.45pm and 6.15-9.45pm. Telephone: 0798 42424.

---

*R*eturn along the lane, take the waymarked path left before Barnsgate Farm and head uphill to a small gate. Bear half-right along a track to the A283. Cross over, turn right, then left through the first gateway and head straight across field towards a tree and a track beyond. Bear right past barns, enter woodland, then at a crossroads of tracks turn right, eventually reaching a lane. Turn left uphill, then at a junction bear right, cross the lane onto a bridleway, then at a crossroads of tracks turn right to reach a lane. Turn right uphill, then just beyond River View Lodge turn left alongside a hedge to a stile. Head straight across pasture, bearing half-right along the line of telegraph poles and through two gates to a lane. Turn right through Little Bognor and turn left along the driveway to Little Bognor Orchard. Take the waymarked path right, then keep left-handed along a field edge to a stile and follow a narrow path through hedgerow into an open field. Keep right-handed, bear left with field edge, then follow waymarker across the field into a copse. Cross two stiles, follow a path to a stile, then bear left to a gate and a lane. Turn right, keep right at A283, cross over onto the lane towards the church and soon bear off right onto a path which leads you back to the car park.

Black Horse,
Byworth, Petworth - village signposted from A283, east of Petworth.

FURTHER EXPLORATION
Petworth House,
Petworth. Magnificent late 17th-century house in a beautiful deer park surrounded by a 13-mile wall. The imposing 320ft west front faces the lake and park and the interior features a collection of pictures (Turner and Van Dyck), sculpture and furniture. Fine carved room with lovely decorations by Grinling Gibbons. (National Trust). House open: April to October, Park daily all year. Telephone 0798 42207.

*N*ORTHIAM ~to~ *E*WHURST GREEN

APPROXIMATELY 5½ MILES

A pleasant, gently undulating walk across farmland, with good views over the Rother Valley

Parking
OS Map 199 Ref TQ8224. Large free car park near the church in Northiam.

White Dog Inn
Ewhurst Green, near Bodiam. Off A229 south of Bodiam.

*F*rom the car park cross the A28, turn left, then right along a waymarked path to Mill Corner and Ewhurst. At a gate bear right (yellow arrow) to follow a grassy path to a footbridge, then keep along the field edge, shortly to cross the centre of a field on a defined track to a crossroads of paths. Turn left, cross a stile by a fingerpost, then head towards a bungalow to a stile and path beside a track. At a drive, turn right, then left along a lane, to a T-junction. Turn right, then immediately left, onto a waymarked path (can be overgrown) into an large field. Bear half-right to the far right-hand corner, crossing a lane by two stiles. At first keep right-handed, then bear half-left downhill to a stile and enter woodland. An ill-defined path drops down to cross a brook, then keep left along the edge of the right-hand gully at a fork of channels, shortly to pick up a path, after passing some fallen tree trunks. Keep right, enter a campsite and keep on past the toilet block and play area before going through a wooden gate on the right. Turn left along fencing, go through the next gate, then bear half-right to a stile in the field corner and turn left along the lane. Shortly, turn right onto a path through young trees to a stile, then bear right round a pond to a wooden footbridge. Climb rough ground, then follow the right-hand field edge before taking a defined cross-field path towards Ewhurst church.

Pass through a field entrance, cross a brook, then turn left along a track and cross another field to a footbridge. Keep left uphill, cross the second stile on the right, then beyond a gate and two more stiles, turn right along a drive, keeping ahead at a lane into Ewhurst. At the T-junction turn right for the pub.

☙ *White Dog Inn* (Free House) ❧

Peacefully set near the village church on a ridge overlooking Bodiam Castle, this old tile-hung pub has an open-plan interior with partly panelled walls, pew seating and a huge brick fireplace. The comfortable eating area is furnished with pine tables. Children are welcome and guest bedrooms are available.

On draught: Bass, Fullers London Pride, Harveys Best Bitter, Boddingtons, Guinness, Fosters, Kronenbourg, Carling Black Label,

Food: the daily menu may include popular pies - pork and Stilton, poacher's (£4.75) - halibut parcels with provençal sauce (£6.95), sirloin steak (£9.50 and supreme of chicken Dijon (£5.50). Puddings (£1.80) range from apple pie to tiramisu. There is also a traditional Sunday lunch (£6.95).

Times: 12-2pm and 7-9.30pm. No food Sun and Mon evenings, light snacks only Mon lunchtime. Telephone: 0580 830264.

From the pub turn left, then right onto a waymarked path, Sussex Border Path, following it downhill to a footbridge and fingerpost on your left. Keep straight on along right-hand edge of field and orchard beyond, leaving it via a footbridge in the corner, then bear left round the field edge to join a lane. Turn right, shortly to rejoin the Border path arrowed along a worn grassy track through pasture to a footbridge. Turn left, then bear off right along a path to a further footbridge and follow it uphill across three pastures to cross a cattle grid onto the driveway past Great Dixter. Keep right back to A28, following it right back to the car park.

FURTHER EXPLORATION

Great Dixter, Northiam
Sir Edwin Lutyens restored this 15th-century house with its notable great hall and laid out the fine gardens. Open Apr to early Oct. Telephone: 0797 253160.

Bodiam Castle, Bodiam
A picture-book moated castle built in 1385 and a favourite with children. The outer walls are virtually complete and the floors have been replaced in some of the towers to allow access to the battlements. Tea room, shop and museum. Open all year. Telephone: 058083 436.

Kent and Sussex Railway, Tenterden-Northiam
Sixteen steam engines make the seven-mile journey through attractive countryside on this re-opened classic branch line, and there are also special events. Telephone: 0580 765155, talking timetable: 0580 762943.

Smallhythe Place, Smallhythe
Dating from Tudor times, this former harbour-master's house became actress Dame Ellen Terry's last home. It is now a museum of memorabilia and the old barn now houses a theatre. (National Trust). Open Apr-Oct. Telephone 05806 2334

*I*DE HILL ~to~ *T*OYS HILL

APPROXIMATELY 4 MILES

This is a rather hilly and strenuous walk, rewarded by some outstanding views over the Kentish countryside and Bough Beech reservoir. Look out for foxes.

Parking
OS Map 188 Ref TQ4851. Good parking area on B2042 south of Ide Hill.

Fox and Hounds
Toys Hill, near Westerham. South of A25 in Brasted.

FURTHER EXPLORATION

Chartwell (2 miles south of Westerham)
The former home of Sir Winston Churchill is filled with reminders of the great statesman, including paintings and other works by notable artists. The garden has walls and ponds laid out by Churchill himself. (National Trust) Telephone: 0732 866368.

Emmett's Garden, Brasted
Charming hillside shrub garden noted for bluebells in spring

Turn left from the parking area along the road for a short distance, then take the No Through Road on the right, signed Greensand Way. Keep to this road, ignoring the Greensand Way route left, and descend to its end by Boar Hill Farm. Turn right onto a path by some garages, climb a stile, turn right, then bear left across a meadow to a stile in the left-hand corner. Cross another meadow to a stile by Chain Farm, then follow the farm drive to a road. Turn left downhill, then turn right by Henden Lodge onto the driveway leading to Henden Manor. Pass to the left of the manor, continue through the farm buildings, shortly to turn right in front of farm cottages onto a concrete track, which becomes a gravel track leading to a stile by a gate and stream. Cross the field ahead, pass through a gap in the hedge, cross another small stream and proceed over two stiles into a meadow. Bear diagonally right to a stile in the top corner, then turn left following the path to a road by a bungalow. Turn right uphill, then soon turn right across a stile into a field. Follow the waymarker to a gate and continue towards houses to a gate onto a driveway, turning left to join a road. Turn right uphill, fork left up a track, then at a crossroads of tracks (blue markers), take the left-hand one uphill to a road. Turn right for the pub.

From the pub, retrace your steps back to the crossroads of blue waymarked tracks. Turn left, following the bridleway uphill through woodland, then after some distance, where the wood is fenced to your left, take the footpath right to a stile and enter the National Trust property of Emmetts Garden. Follow the drive straight ahead, passing the tea shop, and continue to the road. Turn right uphill into Ide Hill and turn left at the roundabout to return to the car park.

❧*Fox and Hounds* (*Greene King*)❧

This traditional and unspoilt country pub, isolated beside a lane high up on the wooded Greensand ridge, has become a popular walkers' retreat. Inside, the small and welcoming half-panelled bar has open fires and is cosily furnished with comfortable old sofas and odd tables and chairs. Photographs of regular customers adorn the walls. There is a pretty garden and a verandah where customers can drink in the summer and children are welcome here, but are not allowed in the bar.

On draught: Greene King IPA and Abbot Ale, Guinness, Harp, Dry Blackthorn cider.
Food: the pub does simple bar snacks only at lunchtime, and there is a small menu of cold dishes like ploughman's and cheese or ham rolls.
Times: (food) 12-2.30pm only. Telephone: 0732 750238.

and fine autumn colours. (National Trust). Telephone: 073275 367

Quebec House, Westerham
General Wolfe spent his childhood at this 16th-century brick house. It contains a museum and an exhibition on his Quebec campaign. (National Trust). Telephone: 0959 562206.

Squerryes Court, Westerham
A fine manor house built in about 1681 and containing a collection of pictures, china, tapestries and furniture.It overlooks a lake and attractive grounds. Telephone: 0959 562345 and 563118.

SHIPBOURNE ~to~ HAMPTONS

APPROXIMATELY 5½ MILES

A very pleasant easy walk through a delightful mixture of orchards and woodland in a beautiful part of Kent.

Parking

OS Map 188 Ref TQ5952. Shipbourne church or on the green opposite.

*C*ross the main road into Upper Green Road, then after about 200 yards turn right across the green to cross a stile in the hedge. Proceed across a field to another stile and turn left along a road, shortly to follow the footpath right before reaching an oast house. Soon cross a stream, climb some steps and turn right to follow the path through woodland. At a pond turn left up a wide forest track and turn left at a crossroads of tracks. Shortly, take a right fork, then on reaching a T-junction turn left, following the track to a Forestry Commission car park. Turn left along the road and take the arrowed footpath right before a white house. Bear left with a yellow waymarker and continue to a field. Turn left along the field edge, then bear right by the yellow marker to a stile. Cross another field and footbridge over a stream to pass by a pylon to a stile and gate onto a road. Turn right uphill, keeping left into Park Road for the pub.

⊰Artichoke Inn *(Free House)*⊱

Originally built in 1483, this attractive white-painted cottage stands on a peaceful lane in the depths of the Kentish countryside. Two welcoming and atmospheric bars have low beams, and are warmed by real fires. An inglenook fireplace is a feature. Wooden settles and farmhouse chairs form the seating and the bars are decorated with gleaming brass, old pictures and other bric-a-brac. Children are welcome in the snug bar if eating.
On draught: Fullers London Pride, Greene King Abbot Ale, Young's Special, guest ales, Heineken, Stella Artois, Young's Premium, Strongbow cider.
Food: the choice includes ploughman's (£3.75), lasagne (£5.50), steak and kidney pie and cod fillet (both £5.95), pork in cider and Barnsley pork chop (both £6.95).
Times: 12-2pm and 7-9.30pm. The restaurant is open for dinner only, 7-9.30pm, Fri and Sat only. Pub closed Sun evening Oct to Etr. Telephone: 0732 810763.

FURTHER EXPLORATION

Old Soar Manor, Plaxtol
Built by the famous Kent family, the Culpepers, in 1290, and amazingly intact, the medieval remains are joined to a lovely Georgian farmhouse. (National Trust) Open daily Apr to Sep.

Ightham Mote, Ightham
A beautiful medieval moated manor house with later additions. Features include the Great Hall, Old Chapel and crypt (1340), and a Tudor chapel with a painted ceiling Open Apr to Oct. Telephone: 0732 810378.

Great Comp Gardens, Borough Green
This 7-acre garden has notable collections of shrubs, trees, heathers and herbaceous plants. Concerts and other events in summer. Open daily Apr to Oct. Telephone: 0732 882669 and 886154.

---

*F*rom the pub take the footpath opposite, signed Roughway and Plaxtol. Cross a footbridge and follow the path along the right-hand field edge to join the waymarked Greensand Way. Cross a footbridge and continue uphill, passing the orchard on the left, to a stile in the right-hand corner. Follow yellow markers across a field to a stile by an oast house and take the drive onto the road. Turn left, pass Roughway Farm, then at a T-junction by the Kentish Rifleman pub turn left and shortly follow the Greensand Way route arrowed right. At a stile with a large stone, cross, and head diagonally across a field to another stile leading into woodland. Pass through the wood to a stile, cross a road and take the farm road towards Fairlawne Home Farm. Pass the farm buildings onto a track, cross a stream and continue uphill to a stile and a road. Turn right back to the church and your car.

ᴅODDINGTON ~to~ ᴇASTLING

**APPROXIMATELY
4½ MILES**

*A pleasant walk
through woods and
across pastures.*

Parking
OS Map 178 Ref TQ9357.
Outside or in the field opposite
Doddington church.

Carpenters Arms
Eastling, near Faversham. Off
A251 south of M2 junction 6.

ake the road and path to the right of the church to
a kissing gate, then bear left across a field to a
stile and cross a driveway. Continue to an iron gate
and join a track through Sharsted Wood (waymarked).
Pass to the right of Sharsted Court, then take the left
fork to follow yellow markers around the edge of an
orchard to rejoin the farm road by a barn. Shortly, turn
right onto a footpath leading to a house. Pass to its
right, then on reaching a private concrete drive at the
edge of an orchard, turn left and descend a wide grass
track to a road. Continue on the footpath opposite,
following it left, then uphill through woodland. On
reaching a clearing keep right through another wood
with a fence on your right. Disregard a stile on your
right and proceed downhill through the wood passing
another footpath and stile on your right. Bear left
through a copse, eventually reaching a walled footpath
(Galvanised Alley). Follow it over two stiles to a road
and turn right for the pub.

◦Carpenters Arms (Shepherd Neame)◦

This small brick and weatherboard pub dates back to 1380 and is full of character. The one cosy bar has a large inglenook fireplace, low beams, wooden pews and chairs round old dining-room tables, and collections of old photographs and bottles. Children are welcome in the delightful little restaurant. There is a garden and three attractive guest bedrooms.

On draught: Shepherd Neame Spitfire, Master Brew and Masons Dark Ale, Beamish, Hurlimans, Steinbock.
Food: bar meals include a hearty soup (£1.50), Carpenters countryman - local sausage and cheese with bread and salad (£4.50) and ploughman's (£2.95). Restaurant fare ranges from salmon steak (£8.75) and breast of duck (£8.95) to fillet steak (£9.95); booking is advisable. Traditional Sunday lunch.
Times: 12-2.30pm (1.30pm Sun) and 6.30-10pm (except Sun evening). Telephone: 079589 0234.

On leaving the pub, turn right along the road and take the farm road on the right just before a large white house (Tonge Farm). Keep to the main path ahead and cross two fields to a road. Climb the stile opposite, cross a field to a stile and continue straight on, heading for the gap between two woods to reach a road. Follow the road opposite, signposted Doddington and descend the hill to follow a waymarked footpath on your right. On reaching a road, just below the 30mph signs, turn left and take the first right uphill back to the church and your car.

Doddington Place Gardens, Doddington
Ten acres of tranquil gardens include displays of rhododendrons and azaleas, a gift shop and a restaurant. Open Etr to Sep. Telephone: 079586 385.

Faversham
Once a flourishing port, this quiet old market town includes many interesting houses, particularly in Court Street and Abbey Street . In the 16th-century Fleur de Lis Heritage Centre a thousand years of history and architecture in Faversham are shown in award-winning displays and an audio-visual programme. Open daily all year. Telephone: 0795 534542.

GODMERSHAM ~to~ CHILHAM

APPROXIMATELY 5½ MILES

A most enjoyable ramble through parkland and farmland and across meadows, which are abundant with wild flowers in May. Splendid views across the Stour Valley.

Parking

OS Map 179 Ref TR0650. Limited parking in village or in the layby with phone box where the walk route crosses the A28.

White Horse

The Square, Chilham Village signposted off A252 between Charing and Canterbury.

FURTHER EXPLORATION

Chilham

One of Kent's most picturesque villages with a central square surrounded by black and white half-timbered houses and an interesting 15th-century flint church. The spacious gardens of Chilham Castle (house not open), with terraces, herb and rose gardens, woodland and

From Godmersham church turn right along the lane and shortly cross the A28 into The Street. Pass under the railway bridge, turn left, then just beyond Valence Dere house bear left onto a waymarked footpath and climb to a line of trees. Go through the trees and continue uphill to join the path to the left at the top of the field. In a few yards turn right through a hedge, turn left and follow the left-hand edge of a field to a stile. Descend to Woodsdale Farm, crossing the stile in the far corner onto a track and pass some garages on your right. Shortly, follow the footpath left, cross three stiles and continue uphill to a stile in the left-hand corner of a field. Pass through a wood, climb another stile and take the path opposite along the field edge and later along the fringe of woodland. At a junction of paths, keep left (Stour Valley Walk) and follow a hedged path, soon to bear right at a fork uphill to a stile. Continue across a meadow, bear left with a marker and shortly turn right between trees to follow markers to a stile and a wide track. Turn right, then cross a stile on the left (marked Link path), where the track curves right. Follow Stour Valley Walk markers and cross a bridge by a mill, a level crossing and the A28 , then follow the lane ahead to Chilham. Bear right by the Woolpack uphill into the square for the pub.

⊷ White Horse *(Whitbread)* ⊶

An attractive and popular 15th-century inn overlooking the centre of this beautiful village. The two comfortable adjoining bars feature low beams and a huge inglenook fireplace with a Lancastrian rose carved at the end of its mantlebeam. During restorations in 1956 two skeletons were found under the floor and are now buried in the neighbouring churchyard. Children are not allowed inside the pub, but there is a small walled and shady beer garden.

On draught: Flowers Original, Wadworth 6X, Fremlins Bitter, Murphy's Stout, Heineken, Stella Artois, Strongbow cider, local Chilham fruit wines.

Food: a snack lunch menu lists soup (£1.60), salads (from £3.60), country platters (from £2.75) and sandwiches (from £1.50) and a changing blackboard menu may feature steak and kidney pie (£4.20), vegetable curry (£3.95), lentil crumble and mushroom stroganoff (both £4.20). There is a separate evening menu.

Times: (food) 12-2.30pm (4pm summer) and 7-9pm (10pm Fri and Sat). No bar food Tue evenings in winter. Pub open 11am-11pm. Telephone: 0227 730355.

---

*T*urn left down School Hill by the entrance to Chilham Castle and proceed along Mountain Street. At the end of the road go through a wooden gate (North Downs Way), then, where the track bears right, climb the stile ahead and follow a track into a fenced area. Follow waymarkers to turn left before Godmersham Park House, and then to the main entrance gate. Turn right along the lane to return to the church and the starting point of the walk.

lakeside walks can be visited. There is also a Raptor Centre, where birds of prey can be seen. Flying displays in the afternoons (except Mon and Fri). Gardens open daily Apr to Oct. Telephone: 0227 730319.

Godmersham Place (not open)

Built by Thomas Brodnax in 1732, the property was later inherited by his cousin, Edward Knight, who was one of Jane Austen's brothers. Jane Austen herself used to stay here and may have used the house and park as a model for estates described in her novels.

ᏝITTLEBOURNE ~to~ ᖴORDWICH

**APPROXIMATELY
6 MILES**

*An easy, mainly level
walk through
woodland and across
meadow and arable
land around the
attractive Stour
Valley.*

Parking
OS Map 179 Ref TQ2157.
In the layby on the right of the
Littlebourne to Wickhambreaux
road

Fordwich Arms
Fordwich, near Canterbury. Off
A28 in Sturry, east of
Canterbury.

FURTHER EXPLORATION

Fordwich
Once the port for Canterbury
on the River Stour, but now the
river is navigable only by
canoe. St Mary's Church has a
sculptured tomb in which, it is
said, the body of St Augustine
once lay. The ancient town hall
is the smallest in the country
and preserves a medieval
ducking-stool.

From the layby, follow the footpath opposite and shortly turn right to the church. Walk along a private road to the right of the church to a stile, then keep right, crossing several stiles to join a road. Opposite the white mill turn left through a gate, cross the stile immediately on your right and keep to the right-hand edge of fields towards Wickhambreaux church. Pass through the churchyard to a kissing gate onto the village green, then turn left up the road, bearing left again, signposted Fordwich. At a T-junction cross the stile ahead and bear left downhill to a stile and footbridge in the left-hand corner of a field. Go on uphill to a road by a bungalow. Turn left, then, on reaching a junction, cross a stile on the right, waymarked Fordwich. Bear diagonally left across a field to cross two stiles just above a farmhouse, then cross a stile on the right, enter woodland and follow markers into Fordwich and the pub.

ᴥ*Fordwich Arms (Whitbread)*ᴥ

Built 63 years ago on the site of the old pub that burnt down in 1928, this handsome Tudor-style pub enjoys a fine setting beside the River Stour. The large bar is decorated with a collection of copper jugs and china plates. Children are welcome in the dining room and outside there is a good riverside seating area.

On draught: Fremlins Bitter, Marston's Pedigree, Boddingtons Bitter, Murphy's, Heineken, Scrumpy Jack and Strongbow cider.

Food: menu includes ploughman's (from £3.20) and salads (from £4.30), sandwiches (from £1.85) and filled baked potatoes (from £3.35). Hot dishes may include moussaka (£5.25), smoked haddock au gratin, smoked chicken and bacon in a mushroom sauce (both £5.95) and a home-made soup (£1.60).

Times: 12-2pm and 6.30-10pm (except Sun evening). Telephone: 0227 710444.

*T*urn right out of the pub car park, then left onto the main village road. Where the road bends right, take the footpath left along a grass bank to a stile. Follow the track to cross another stile on the right into a tree plantation and proceed between trees to a junction of tracks. Continue straight on, bear left and shortly take the footpath through the trees to a stile in the top left-hand corner. Head uphill into woodland to a wooden gate and cross a playing field, keeping to the right of the clubhouse to a road. Turn left, then cross the stile on the right just before Trenley Lodge and follow the path through Trenley Woods to a crossroads of tracks. Turn right downhill, cross a small stream and continue on the worn track into a clearing, then bear left into another wood. Soon cross a road, take the path by an iron gate and pass a pond on the right to join a metalled drive. Proceed for some distance, pass through an iron gate, then where the drive bears left, take the farm track right which leads down to Littlebourne playing field. Walk down the left-hand side of the field, then either turn left onto the footpath to the church or continue ahead back at the layby.

Howletts Zoo Park, Bekesbourne

One of John Aspinall's animal collections, containing the world's largest breeding gorilla colony. Tigers, small cats, deer, antelope, snow leopards, bison, endangered species of monkey and Britain's only herd of breeding elephants can be seen. Open daily all year. Telephone: 0227 721286.

Stodmarsh National Nature Reserve

Located a couple of miles up the Stour Valley, this is an important reserve for breeding birds with various lakes and reedbeds. On the Stour Valley Walk.

ƑRENSHAM ~to~ ƇILFORD

APPROXIMATELY 6 MILES

A varied walk across heathland, beside ponds and rivers and through woodland, offering delightful views of densely wooded hills. A good birdwatching area, so take your binoculars. Soft sandy paths can make the going difficult.

Ｌeave the car park, keeping Frensham Great Pond on your right, bear left at end of the pond to a road, and at the bus stop cross over onto a footpath and go on to the top of the ridge. Beyond wooden barriers turn left, then at a junction of five paths, follow the footpath to the left of the 'No horses, No cycles' sign, and continue through two wooden barriers, taking the footpath to the right of the second barrier. Descend to Little Frensham Pond crossing all tracks. Keep the pond to your right, bearing left through trees at its end, and turn right before entering the car park. Shortly, cross a road onto a footpath, pass to the left of the public toilets, then at junction of paths turn right and pass Keepers Cottage. Continue over a bridge and through Pierrepont Home Farm. Bear right through a gate and proceed through woodland to a road. Turn right, then on reaching a junction turn right again and shortly turn left, beyond the twin bridges, for the pub.

◈Barley Mow (Courage)◈

Idyllically set by the village cricket green the inn is a very popular destination on summer weekends. The cosy bars have oak beams and in winter months a rear room is allocated to rambling parties. There is an attractive, well-tended riverside garden with a barbecue. Children are not allowed inside.

On draught: Courage Best Bitter and Directors, guest ales, Beamish, Carlsberg, Dry Blackthorn cider.
Food: the inn emphasises good home-cooking with its lunchtime and a separate evening menus; examples are cheddar ploughman's (£3.75), lasagne, steak and kidney pie, fisherman's pie (all £5.50), steaks (£8.50) and lamb noisettes with apricot and ginger sauce (£8)
Times: 12-2pm and 7-9pm. No hot food on Sun. Summer afternoon teas. Telephone: 0252 792205.

———◈———

$\mathcal{T}$urn right on leaving the pub, then on reaching a road cross over onto a waymarked footpath. Beyond a gate bear left, then right and proceed through a gate into woodland. Continue straight ahead with the river on your right then on merging with a sandy path from the left, keep right to reach a stile. Cross over, turn right, and at the first intersection of paths (wooden gate on your right), turn left onto a narrow sandy path (not waymarked) and soon pass a saw mill to reach a road. Bear left, cross over onto a footpath and proceed over all junctions to some houses on your left, then continue with the blue arrow to a road. Turn right, and follow it to the common. Take the grassy track signed 'No horses, No dogs' to the top of a ridge, then descend to cross a road back into the car park.

Parking
OS Map 186 Ref SU8540. Frensham Great Pond car park. Follow signs to Frensham Country Park off A287.

Barley Mow
Tilford. Village signposted off B3001 south-east of Farnham.

FURTHER EXPLORATION

Tilford
Features of this idyllic English village are the green and cricket pitch, on which Tilford Cricket Club have played since 1886 and which has been used for many a TV commercial. Also of interest are two medieval bridges over the River Wey and a huge old oak tree known as King John's Oak, said to be 900 years old.

Museum of Rural Life, Tilford
An old kiln houses a collection of farm implements and machinery and examples of the crafts and trades allied to farming may be seen. In old farm buildings there are a smithy and a wheelwright's shop, hand tools and other artefacts. In the 10 acres of grounds are woodland walks and an arboretum. Open Apr to Sep. Telephone: 025125 2300 and 5571.

ℋOLMWOOD ~to~ 𝒞OLDHARBOUR

**APPROXIMATELY
4 MILES**

*A beautiful
undulating walk
through farmland and
along the Greensand
Ridge near Leith Hill,
with panoramic
views towards the
South Downs from
several vantage
points. A few short
but steep climbs*

eturn along Hawksmoor Drive, turn right, then right again at Beare Green Court and take footpath to the left of Beare Green Stores. Shortly, cross a road into Woodside Road, at the end of which cross a road onto a waymarked footpath. Continue across a wooden bridge and a stile, then left along the field edge for a short distance before bearing right uphill across the field to a track. Cross the track via stiles, keep on, with the pond to your left, and cross the railway line. Stay left-handed along the field edge, cross two stiles in the hedge and maintain direction to pass a farm to a stile and a drive. Turn right, go through gates and turn right into Henshurst Cross Lane. In about 150 yards, take the waymarked path left through woodland to a stile, then with the trees to your left, cross a field to a stile. Bear slightly right uphill across a field to a stile and turn left onto a track, passing Kitlands Cottage. Shortly, turn right onto a poorly signed, steep footpath and go through woodland. Cross a stile, then head downhill to a gate, turning right for the pub.

☙ *Plough Inn (Free House)* ❧

Set among wooded hills in a tiny hamlet, this 350-year-old building is the highest pub in south-east England, standing at almost 1000ft. Popular with walkers and cyclists, the unpretentious bars have an assortment of wooden tables and chairs, and their ochre-coloured walls are decorated with old guns, jugs and plates. There is a good, traditional, pubby atmosphere and there are two letting bedrooms. In summer, the peaceful garden, which has good views, is popular. Children are welcome there, or inside, in the family room and eating area.

On draught: as many as nine real ales, such as Theakston Old Peculier, Morland Old Speckled Hen, Adnams Broadside, Hall and Woodhouse Tanglefoot, Wadworth 6X, Gibbs Mew Bishop's Tipple and Batemans XB, Guinness, Carlsberg, Stella Artois, Biddenden farmhouse cider, country wines.
Food: generous portions of home-cooked food include cottage pie (£4.75), broccoli and Stilton flan (£5.75), steak and kidney pie (£5.95), liver and bacon (£5.25), ploughman's (£3.25), chicken and leek pie (£5.25), filled jacket potatoes (£3.95) and a range of vegetarian dishes, of which a typical example might be cashew and garlic pasta bake (£5.50).
Times: 12-2.30pm and 7.30- 9.30pm Telephone: 0306 711793.

───◆◆◆───

From the pub, turn right uphill, shortly to take the first turning right, then turn left onto a concrete track through Anstiebury Farm. Cross a stile to your right and bear slightly left downhill across a field to a further stile (the ground falls away steeply to your right). Keep left, descending through woodland to a stile, then keep on straight across two fields to a stile in the left-hand corner. Turn left onto a track which leads into Moorhurst Lane. Proceed to a junction with the main road and turn right to get back to Holmwood Station and your car.

Parking
OS Map 187 Ref TQ1743. Holmwood Station or layby in Hawksmoor Drive, the first turning right south of the station.

Plough Inn Coldharbour,
near Dorking. Three miles south-west of Dorking off A24 and A29.

FURTHER EXPLORATION

Leith Hill Tower
An 18th-century tower on the highest point in south-east England. The top of the tower is at 1,029ft above sea-level and provides magnificent views to the North and South Downs. Excellent woodland walks. (National Trust). Tower open Apr to Sep. Telephone: 0306 712434.

Polesden Lacy, Great Bookham
(north-west of Dorking) Attractive Regency house containing the Greville collection of tapestries, porcelain, Old Master paintings and other works of art. Open-air theatre in summer months. (National Trust) Grounds open daily all year; house open Mar to Nov. Telephone: 0372 458203.

$\mathcal{K}$INTBURY
~to~ $\mathcal{H}$AMSTEAD MARSHALL

APPROXIMATELY 6 MILES

A very scenic, easy-going walk along the Kennet and Avon Canal towpath and through unspoilt farmland on well way-marked paths and tracks. Abundant wildlife includes grebes, duck, swans, wagtails and finches.

Parking

OS Map 174 Ref SU3867. Kintbury public car park, near the canal and railway station.

White Hart

Hamstead Marshall, Newbury. The village is signposted off the A4 west of Newbury.

From the car park, turn right, then left on the canal towpath to Hamstead Lock. At the lock and road, turn right to cross canal and river and pass Hamstead Mill. Climb a stile, left, and bear right onto a tree-lined track, curving right to the church. At a waymarker, turn left to a stile, bear half-left across pasture, go through a gateway, then on to a stile and down to a kissing gate. Cross the lane, go through a gate, take the bridleway over a field to a gate. Go between farm buildings. At the road turn left for the pub.

⟿ White Hart *(Free House)* ↶

This old village inn is Italian owned and has a separate restaurant. The delightful garden is full of roses and a barn conversion houses six guest bedrooms.

On draught: Wadworth 6X, Hall and Woodhouse Badger Best, Murphy's.
Food: home-made pasta dishes are a speciality (all £6.50); other dishes include grilled goat's cheese with garlic and yoghurt (£4.50), meatballs stuffed with mozzarella in a wine sauce (£7.90) and lemon sole grilled with pesto (£8.50).
Times: 12-2pm and 7-10pm. Closed Sun and 3 weeks in Aug. Telephone: 0488 58201.

Turn right from the pub, right at the next junction, then shortly take an arrowed path left over a stile. Bear half-left to a stile, turn left onto a track, then right at a T-junction and follow the track to a lane. Turn left, pass Pear Tree Cottage, and take the waymarked path right to a gate. Head diagonally left uphill between two trees to a stile in the corner. Continue to a stile by a gate onto a track, bearing left to a cattle grid, through a gate on the right and downhill to a stile. Cross the canal bridge and go left along the towpath for Kintbury.

ᴇAST ILSLEY ~to~ ᴡEST ILSLEY

From the Swan, cross the road into a T-road and shortly take the bridleway on your right. This wide track becomes grassy, gently climbs uphill and eventually crosses a gallop to a junction of tracks. Turn left and follow Ridgeway signs along the crest of the down. Pass beneath A34, take the second waymarked track left, keep right-handed past gallops and a bridleway post to follow the track downhill, skirting a copse, to the lane. Turn right and go through the village for the pub.

ᴔHarrow *(Morland)*ᴒ

Standing opposite the pond and cricket pitch, this friendly country inn is furnished in traditional style, with outdoor benches overlooking the cricket pitch. Children are welcome.

On draught: Morland Original, Old Masters and Old Speckled Hen, Guinness.
Food: hearty country cooking includes splendid pies - rabbit, and steak and mushroom (both £4.85) and venison (£5.75). Other dishes range from filled granary rolls to lamb's liver and bacon (£6.95) or aubergine and potato gratin (£4.50) and good ploughman's (from £4.50).
Times: 12- 2pm and 6 (7pm Sun)-9.15pm. Telephone: 0635281 260.

Retrace your steps through the village and turn right along the lane beside the Old Chapel, signed West Ilsley Stables. Bear left with a metalled drive and then right with the waymarker onto a track just before the farm complex. At a junction of paths, keep left, climb gently uphill and follow blue arrows. Keep left at the two forks of arrowed paths, then (red arrow) follow an established path to a lane. Keep on ahead beneath A34 back into East Ilsley.

APPROXIMATELY 6 MILES

A gently undulating downland walk, exploring the Ridgeway Path and established wide tracks with good open farmland views.

Parking
OS Map 174 Ref SU4980. In East Ilsley village, good layby on lane between The Swan and The Crown and Horns.

Harrow
West Ilsley, Newbury. Village signposted off A34, 8 miles north of Newbury.

FURTHER EXPLORATION

Ridgeway Path
Reputedly the oldest highway in Britain, used by primitive man over 4000 years ago and thought to have linked East Anglia to Dorset. The present trail links Ivinghoe Beacon in Buckinghamshire to Avebury, Wiltshire, a distance of 85 miles.

BUCKLEBURY COMMON ~to~ STANFORD DINGLEY

APPROXIMATELY 4½ MILES

A peaceful and varied walk across unspoilt common land, through woodland and alongside the tiny River Pang.

Parking

OS Map 174 Ref SU5569. Free parking area on Bucklebury Common, near the crossroads at Carbinswood Lane.

From the car park, turn right to a crossroads and take the waymarked path beside Carbinswood Lane into the trees. Cross open common to a junction of paths and turn left along a wide track. At a T-junction turn right, pass Heatherwood Kennels, then bear left,and where the track curves left again, keep ahead on a path through woodland. Shortly, bear left onto a gravel drive by houses, then just before reaching the road, bear right onto a path parallel to it. At a track turn left, cross the road, then in 100 yards, at a staggered crossroads of tracks, turn right. By some cottages and a junction of tracks, turn right, then left along a gravel track and soon bear right onto a muddy path along a line of telegraph poles. Cross a grassy area and a lane onto a waymarked bridleway beside a thatched cottage. Keep on at the end of the track on a gentle downhill path to a gate. Follow blue arrow left-handed through pasture, then ignore an arrowed path left and continue to a gate and track. At a lane turn right into the village, then left onto a footpath just beyond the Old Boot Inn, following it to the Bull.

⊷*Bull (Free House)*⊶

The Bull
Stanford Dingley, near Newbury. Follow Bucklebury signs off A4 at Thatcham, cross wooded Bucklebury Common and turn left at Chapel Row, signed to the village.

Dating from the 15th century, this attractive redbrick inn remains delightfully unspoilt with two traditional bars. Dark beams, standing timbers, quarry-tiled floors, scrubbed pine tables, old pews, cushioned benches and open fires characterise the welcoming and relaxing interior. There is also seating outside. Children are welcome in the saloon bar at lunchtime and till 8.30pm, but not Saturday evenings.

On draught: Brakspears Bitter, Bass, guest ale, Guinness, Tennant Extra, Carling Black Label, Dry Blackthorn cider.

Food: reliable home-cooking includes leek, cheese and potato pie (£4.60), curried parsnip soup (£2.30), garlic, bacon and mushrooms on toast (£2.95), drunken fish pie (£4.55), chilli (£4.95), chicken Provençal (£6.45), ploughman's (from £2.75) and filled jacket potatoes (from £1.85).

Times:12-2.30pm and 7-10pm. Closed Monday lunchtime. Telephone: 0734 744409.

FURTHER EXPLORATION

Basildon Park, Upper Basildon

A fine classical 18th-century house, built of golden Bath stone, in a beautiful setting overlooking the Thames Valley. Inside, there are delicate plasterwork decorations on the walls and ceilings, an elegant staircase and the impressive and unusual Octagon drawing room with notable pictures and furniture and three big windows with splendid views. Formal garden and woodland walks. (National Trust) Open Apr to Oct. Telephone: 0734 843040.

***O**n leaving the inn turn right along the lane, shortly to take the waymarked path left, opposite the church. Cross pasture to the River Pang, turn right to a gate and pass through a copse to a stile. Bear half-right to the field corner, turn right along a track to a stile beside a gate. Turn left across this stile and follow the field edge to another one, then keep to the riverside path to the next stile and soon cross a footbridge over the river. Head slightly right across a field to a stile in the hedge and continue ahead on a track between pig fields. Keep straight on at a crossroads of paths, along the field edge to a stile, then bear diagonally right to one in the field corner and a lane. Turn left and shortly bear right onto a bridleway beside a house called Four Seasons. Follow a narrow path uphill through woodland, keeping gardens and properties to your left. At a T-junction with a wide track, turn right and continue over a crossroads of tracks, soon to bear left back to the crossroads near the parking area.

TURVILLE ~to~ IBSTONE

APPROXIMATELY 5 MILES

A splendid rural walk through peaceful valley farmland and Chiltern beech woods.

Parking

OS Map 175 SU7691. Centre of village near church and green.

Fox

Ibstone, near Stokenchurch. Just under 2 miles south of M40 junction 5 at Ibstone Common.

FURTHER EXPLORATION

Turville

An attractive small village, nestling deep in the Chilterns, that has grown little over the past two centuries. The Church of St Mary the Virgin is mainly 14th century, and preserves a medieval stone coffin and an 18th-century chapel with interesting monuments.

Take the waymarked path opposite the green beside the Old School House, bearing off right to a stile, then gradually climb uphill over two stiles before ascending steeply towards Turville Windmill. At the top of the hill, keep right-handed to a stile and lane. Turn right, then left onto a waymarked path through a gate and descend with white arrows through woodland and a pasture to a gate. Almost immediately turn sharp left onto a narrow path that follows the valley bottom. Keep right on, merging with a track, then left, maintaining direction through woodland. At a stile and crossroads of paths, proceed ahead and continue forward where a blue arrow waymarks a path left, then go straight across an established track, shortly to pass a wildlife conservation area. On reaching a crossroads of paths (white arrows), turn left onto a wide track, bearing right uphill through woodland. Emerge onto open grassland, keep right-handed uphill to join a defined path leading to a lane. Turn right, and pass Ibstone Common to find the Fox on your right.

∽*Fox (Free House)*∽

Overlooking the common and beechwoods, this smart 17th-century country inn - although much extended - retains an old-fashioned charm in its relaxing lounge bar, which has low beams, settles, comfortable seating, log fires and old photographs on the walls. Children are welcome in the eating area. Guest bedrooms are available.

On draught: Brakspear Bitter, Marlow Rebellion, Luxters Barn Ale, Greene King Abbot Ale, Stella Artois, Heineken.

Food: a good bar food selection features game pie, steak and kidney pie (both £5.75), pheasant en croûte, poached salmon (both £5.95), steaks (from £7.95), soup (£2.50), farmhouse rolls (from £1.70) and ploughman's (from (£3.25). There is a separate restaurant menu.

Times: 12-2pm and 7-10pm. Telephone: 0491 638289.

From the pub, turn right along a lane, shortly to turn left onto a defined grassy path through bracken and scrub. Pass an old pond, keep left at a track, then proceed right-handed along the edge of Ibstone Common to cross a driveway onto a wide muddy path through trees. At a gravel track keep left past Farside Cottage, then, on reaching a metalled lane, turn right, shortly to take the waymarked path left, opposite Hell Corner Cottage. Head downhill into woodland on a stony path to a T-junction of tracks, turn right to follow a path through beech wood. Before a stile on the woodland edge, bear right, maintaining course on a woodland path, keeping ahead at the next junction and soon bear left through the churchyard onto the drive to Manor Farm. Turn left, then right downhill on a lane, then bear left onto a waymarked scenic path through the woodland edge. As the main path bears left into the wood, turn right towards a field entrance, then follow a narrow path left along the field edge to cross a second stile into pasture. Bear half-left down to the lower stile, pass through scrub and cross three stiles and a field on a defined path, that eventually brings you to Turville. Turn left along the lane to the church and your car.

Ibstone

Recorded in the Domesday Book as Hibestones, the village derives its name from Ibba's Stones. Ibba belonged to the court of King Offa of Mercia, and the 'stones' probably refer to the nearby county boundary. St Nicholas' Church has a beautiful setting and the ancient yew tree in the churchyard is reputed to be as old as the Norman church.

ℱARNHAM COMMON
~to~ℒITTLEWORTH COMMON

**APPROXIMATELY
4 MILES**

*A pleasant walk
through the extensive
and attractive beech
woods of Burnham
Beeches, returning
along open paths and
shady wooded ways.*

Parking
OS Map 175 Ref SU9585. Main
Burnham Beeches car park on
the west side of Farnham
Common.

Blackwood Arms
Common Lane, Littleworth
Common, near Beaconsfield.
Three miles south of M40 off
A355.

FURTHER EXPLORATION

Burnham Beeches
A 600-acre tract of woodland,
purchased by the City of
London in 1879. It is part of a
vast forest that extended over
the Chilterns in prehistoric
times.

𝒲alk west along the open common area in the
front of the parking bays, pass the ice-cream
kiosk and bear right to join the main drive by some
white gates. Keep right, following the metalled drive -
Halse Drive - through the beech woodland to the
Hartley Court Moat sign board and a junction. Where
the drive bears left, proceed straight ahead to join a
woodland path, then cross a lane and a stile to follow
an arrowed defined path (Beeches Way) through
mixed deciduous woodland. Keep left at a fork, shortly
to leave the woodland via a wooden kissing gate. Cross
a meadow to two stiles, then keep left-handed through
pasture to a stile flanking a metal gate. Follow a track
to a further stile and lane, turning right for the pub.

↬*Blackwood Arms* (Free House)↫

This country pub stands in a fine location on the edge
of common land and is a popular destination for
walkers. There is a friendly atmosphere in the simply
furnished single bar which has a real fire. Outside,
there is a splendid rear suntrap garden and terrace
with benches, tables and chairs overlooking fields.
Children are welcome.

On draught: regularly changing selection of ales - Hop
Back Summer Lightning, Adnams Southwold, Timothy
Taylor Landlord, Gibbs Mew Bishop's Tipple, Carling
Black Label, Addlestones and a farmhouse cider.
Food: the menu offers excellent value, from long rolls
with various fillings (from £1.60), ploughman's (£2.50),
cauliflower cheese and garlic bread (£1.95), to steak
and ale pie (£3.25), chicken and cider curry and fish pie
(both £3.50). Evenings specials may be chicken and
mango (£4.25), lamb and herbs (£4.50) and rump steak
(£5.95). Traditional Sunday roast (£4.25)
Times: 12-2pm and 6 (7 Sun)-9.30pm.
Telephone: 0753 642169

*L*eave the pub, turn left, then bear half-right into the car park to take the bridleway leading off it (not the Beeches Way at the far end) through woodland. Turn left on reaching a lane, pass the Beech Tree pub and bear left with the lane to reach a waymarked path over a stile on your right. Keep left-handed around the edge of pasture, first beside woodland, then alongside a tree-lined hedge and pass through the hedge on a narrow path. Proceed along the left-hand edge of three fields to a stile and the end of a hedged path. Turn left through an old gate, then bear left on a defined path across pasture to cross a lane via two stiles. Keep to the right-hand edge of the field, passing Dorney Wood on your right, to a stile beside an electricity sub-station. Turn right along a lane, then bear off left beside the large Burnham Beeches sign to join a worn path that runs parallel to a lane. Eventually join the lane, keep left downhill and turn left at the bottom into Victoria Drive, a delightful path through beech woods. On reaching the main metalled drive turn right, following it back to the main car park.

Cliveden

This palatial mansion, the former home of the Astor family, is now a very grand hotel. Its extensive gardens and woodland and three of the rooms are open to the public. (National Trust). Telephone: 0628 605069.

Bekonscot Model Village, Beaconsfield

A miniature world where time has stood still for over 60 years with a model railway, airfield, castles, mine and new elevated walkway. Open daily Apr to Oct. Telephone: 0494 672919.

$\mathcal{H}$AMBLEDEN ~to~ $\mathcal{F}$AWLEY

APPROXIMATELY
5½ MILES

A peaceful ramble through attractive beech woodland and lush valley pasture in rural Buckinghamshire.

Parking

OS Map 175 Ref SU7886. Free car park in Hambleden village.

Walnut Tree

Fawley, Henley-on-Thames. Off A4155 between Henley and Marlow.

FURTHER EXPLORATION

Greys Court, Henley-on-Thames

This charming gabled house has a 16th-century core and is set amid the remains of the courtyard walls and towers of a fortified house. The gardens include a white garden, a rose garden and a modern 'pattern' maze. (National Trust). Telephone: 04917 529.

From the car park turn left into the village square, keeping ahead between the central tree and church to follow the lane out of village, passing the Old Bakery. Shortly, take the first waymarked route on your right, along a path through valley pasture, passing through two kissing gates, a copse and to the rear of houses. Cross a lane and two pastures beyond, then climb a stile in the left-hand hedge before bearing half-right to a ladder stile in a thick hedgerow. Keep right to another stile, turn left along a lane, then at a T-junction cross over to follow an arrowed path across an arable field towards a house and join a farm track. Continue ahead, the track soon curving right, climbing steadily into woodland. Keep left at a fork, following white arrows, then where the track bears left, keep ahead with arrows along path HA43. Turn right at a junction with a wide track and descend to a crossroads of tracks in a clump of beech trees. Go straight across (white arrows - HA37), and ascend through woodland, the path becoming hedged as it leaves the wood. Climb a stile on the left, cross an open field, keep left and soon pass through a small wooden gate on your right and head towards Lower Woodend Farm. Follow its drive to a lane and turn left for the pub.

$\backsim$*Walnut Tree* (Brakspear)$\backsim$

Tucked down a country lane, this smart, modern pub is a popular dining venue. There are public and lounge bars, with an adjoining garden room housing the restaurant. Outside are a large patio and an attractive, spacious garden with rural views. Children are welcome in eating areas. Guest bedrooms are available.
On draught: Brakspear Bitter and Special, Guinness, Stella Artois, Strongbow, good selection of wines.
Food: bar menu includes coarse country pâté (£2.95), smoked salmon and trout mousse (£3.95), steak and kidney pie (£4.75), Cumberland sausage and bacon casserole (£3.95), stuffed aubergines (£4.50), home-

made burger (£5.75) and walnut and treacle tart and hot apple pie (both £2.50) for pudding. More elaborate dishes, especially fresh fish, are available in the restaurant. Afternoon teas are served in summer.
Times: 12-2pm (2.30pm weekends) and 7-10pm. Telephone: 049163 8360.

*R*eturn along the lane to where it bends left and take a bridleway between Roundhouse Farm and Meadowsweet Cottage. On reaching a white gate and driveway to Orchards, bear off right onto a narrow path that soon enters woodland. Follow a white arrow, keeping right where a track converges from your left, then go left at the next junction and remain on the main track, shortly to leave the wood on a trackway through grassland. At a junction turn right along a stony track, then shortly turn left along a narrow waymarked path which follows the woodland fringe, eventually bearing left down to a wide track, beside houses, to a road. Turn right, cross over and turn left onto a trackway, following it past a barn, then left at a junction, shortly to pass the recreation ground and tennis courts. Pass through a kissing gate on the left and bear half-right across a playing field back to the car park.

Stonor House and Park, Stonor

Home of Lord and Lady Camoys, the house dates back to 1180. It has preserved a medieval Catholic chapel and some of the earliest domestic architecture in the county. The building's treasures include rare furniture, paintings, sculptures and tapestries. The house is set in beautiful gardens and has a delightful deer park. Telephone: 0491 638587.

DORCHESTER-ON-THAMES ~to~ CLIFTON HAMPDEN

APPROXIMATELY 6 MILES

Delightful riverside walk along the banks of the River Thames passing Day's Lock. Plenty of wildlife.

Parking
OS Map 164 Ref SU5794. Free car park just south of the village centre.

Plough Inn
Clifton Hampden. South of A415 towards Long Wittenham.

FURTHER EXPLORATION

Dorchester-on-Thames
A beautiful small town on the Thames with a history dating back to the Bronze Age and once an important Roman settlement. The old High Street is winding and lovely, lined with half-timbered or brick houses and a late-Norman abbey with 13th-century glass.

From the car park turn left along the village lane, passing the Roman Catholic church, then bear off right, and join a track waymarked left to the river and Long Wittenham. At the end of the houses, proceed ahead on a well worn path to a stile. Ignore the path over the stile, instead follow the field edge with ancient dykes to your left. Shortly, the path narrows and leads you to a small wooden gate, then bear half-right across pasture to a metal swing gate and cross Day's Lock and the weir. Turn right onto the riverbank, and follow it via a series of gates and stiles to Clifton Hampden. At the lane, turn right, cross the Thames, and keep on to the traffic lights and junction with A415. The Plough lies opposite.

Plough Inn *(Free House)*

This thatched village pub has kept its old beams and panelling, and both the bar and separate restaurant are beautifully furnished. Guests receive a friendly welcome from the hospitable Turkish owners. Outside there is a large garden and overnight accommodation is available in a delightful four-poster bedroom. Children are very welcome.

On draught: Courage Best Bitter, Ruddles County, Websters Yorkshire Bitter, Fosters, Kronenbourg,.
Food: good home-cooked bar food is available all day, ranging from soup (£2.45), and sandwiches (from £2.25), to warm salad of smoked chicken (£4.50), moussaka (£4.95), kebabs (£5.95), steak and beer pie (£5.25) Puddings include baclava and bread and butter pudding (both £2.45). There is a set menu at £14.50.
Times: 11am- 11pm. Telephone: 0865 407811

The return route retraces your steps along the idyllic riverside path back to Dorchester-on-Thames.

ℒONG COMPTON
~to~ ℒITTLE COMPTON

ocate the village store and walk along the driveway to the side of it (not waymarked), which soon becomes a track. It gradually climbs uphill, to a group of barns. Here turn right, heading west, to pass a house and more barns. At the road, cross, go over the field ahead and turn left to go down a grassy slope to Little Compton, emerging almost at the back of the Red Lion.

⮞Red Lion Inn (Donnington)⮜

This charming 16th-century village inn has a large public bar and a low-ceilinged lounge bar with exposed stone walls, beams, and a stone fireplace. There is a pleasant garden and children are also welcome in the dining area. Three guest bedrooms are available. No dogs - even in the garden.

On draught: Donnington BB and SBA, Guinness.

Food: food ranges from bar snacks such as filled granary rolls, pâté and various ploughman's to smoked salmon and prawn creole (£4.95) and pheasant casserole (£6.25). Separate restaurant menu.

Times: 12-2pm (1.15pm Sun) and 7-8.45pm (9.30pm Sat). Telephone: 060874 397.

rom the inn turn left, then left again towards the church, and at Reed Cottage right onto a lane, signed Barton-on-the-Heath. At the cemetery bear right on a waymarked path across a field, then follow the river (can be mudddy) to the end of the next field and turn left towards a farm. Bear right over a ditch, then left and walk through the yard, keeping the farmhouse to your left before turning right at a barn. Now retrace the outward route as far as the group of barns, then bear right uphill on a track towards the radio/TV mast. At the end of the track, beyond a metal gate, and with Long Compton in sight, turn left along the field edge, bearing right to South Hill Farm. Keep ahead downhill back to Long Compton.

APPROXIMATELY 6 MILES

This is an enjoyable and easy walk, mainly along firm wide bridleways, with outstanding views across rolling hills and valleys. Although some uphill is involved the route is not too demanding.

Start of Walk
OS Map 15 Ref SP2832. Off A34 in Long Compton, at the village store.

Red Lion
Little Compton, Moreton-in-Marsh - off A44, 4 miles north-west of Chipping Norton.

FURTHER EXPLORATION

Rollright Stones
This Bronze-Age stone circle, known as the King's Men, lies on the ridge south of Long Compton. Legend has it that the king and his knights were turned to stone by a witch.

*R*ATLEY ~to~ *W*ARMINGTON

**APPROXIMATELY
5 MILES**

*A fairly energetic, but
not too demanding,
walk through
farmland and
downland affording
good open views.*

Parking
OS Map 151 Ref SP3847.
Ratley village hall.

Plough
Warmington, Banbury - just off
B4100 north of Banbury.

FURTHER EXPLORATION

Edgehill
This is the site of the first
major Civil War battle in
October 1642, when
Parliament's army, commanded
by Robert Devereaux, 3rd Earl
of Essex, clashed with the
Royalist army commanded by
King Charles I. Thirty thousand
men fought in this battle.
Models and dioramas can be
seen at the nearby Edgehill
Battle Museum at
Farnborough. Telephone: 0295
89593.

*M*ake your way to the Rose and Crown pub and turn right into Featherbow Lane, looking out for a stile on your right. A yellow arrow directs you downhill across pasture to another stile, then through a field to a gate. Cross a brook and head up the valley side, keeping to the right of a communications mast and to the left of a water tower, along a track into Hornton Hill Farm. In the farmyard, turn left onto a grassy bridleway, then at the next junction bear left to follow a well defined undulating track across sheep-covered downland into Fir Tree Farm and out to the B4100. Turn left, cross the road to join a footpath beside Warmington church into the village and the pub which lies to the left close to the green.

*F*rom the pub turn right and pass the church to reach the main road. Turn right, then after 50 yards turn left across a stile to follow the waymarked ill-defined path downhill to a distant stile. Keep to the field edge to a ditch, cross over and turn immediately left and right, then with the hedge to your right proceed ahead soon to cross a further ditch before reaching a stile. Head across pasture towards a house called Arlescote, go through a farm gate and pass in front of the house and its splendid wall to rejoin the footpath opposite the entrance to Primrose Farm. Pass through sheep pastures and climb steeply up an oak-covered slope, with far-reaching views across Warwickshire countryside, then on reaching the top cross the road and make for the prominent wooden bridge in front of you. Turn left and bear right around a field, then head across the next field to a stile and so back into Ratley.

☙*Plough* (Free House)❧

An unpretentious 17th-century, stone-built village pub with a cosy beamed bar, furnished with dark wooden pews, cushioned wall seats and chairs in front of a good log fire. Children are welcome in the bar.

On draught: Hook Norton Best Bitter, Old Hookey, Marston's Pedigree, guest ale, McEwan Export, Guinness, Stella Artois, Heineken, Woodpecker, Bulmer's Original cider.

Food: generously served lunchtime fare includes sandwiches (£1), ploughman's at (£2.95), home-cooked ham, egg and chips (£4.75), scampi and chips (£4.50), soup, cottage pie and home-made daily specials (from £3.50). Children's portions (£1.95).

Times: 12-2pm only. Telephone: 029589 666.

Warmington

A most attractive unspoilt village of golden ironstone houses clustered around a green. St Michael's Church has changed little over the centuries In the churchyard a headstone commemorates a Captain Alexander Gourdin who was killed at the Battle of Edgehill.

Upton House

Mellow stone house dating from 1695 and containing outstanding collections of paintings by English and Continental Masters, Brussels tapestries, Sèvres porcelain and 18th-century furniture. Fine gardens. (National Trust) Telephone: 029587 266.

CHEDWORTH ~to~ FOSSEBRIDGE

**APPROXIMATELY
5½ MILES**

*A fairly easy going
walk over rolling
country, which
combines open rural
views, woodland and
valley paths and
attractive village
streets.*

Start of walk
OS Map 163 SP0512
Chedworth Church.

Fossebridge Inn
Fossebridge
Northleach. On A429 5 miles
north of Cirencester

FURTHER EXPLORATION

Chedworth Roman Villa
Some of the best preserved
Roman remains in Britain can
be seen here. The villa dates
from AD180 and displays some
30 rooms, baths, mosaics and
a shrine. Telephone: 0242
890256

With the church to your left walk along the lane to a stile and footpath waymarked to the Roman Villa, then cross the hollow pasture to the next stile and climb the stepped slope, continuing straight on at the top through a gate. Turn immediately right through a second gate to follow the path between a stone wall and a fence, bearing left at the end along a track (not signed). A fingerpost soon directs you across a large field (may be under crop) with good views, then on entering another field, head gently downhill towards two solitary trees. On reaching them, bear left downhill to join an undulating track through mixed woodland, following yellow arrows (you will find them at waist height) to a road. Cross the river to Yanworth Mill and rejoin the footpath opposite the mill, following the grassy path alongside the walls of Stowell Park to a wooden gate. Turn right through a second gate and walk parallel to the stream to a road, cross over, then head straight on gently climbing uphill through parkland with woodland to your right. Shortly, enter pasture, turn half-right uphill towards the sound of traffic, then at the top bear right to descend first through woodland, then steeply across pasture to a green gate and the road by the Fossebridge Inn

Fossebridge Inn (Free House)

Originally a coaching inn, this appealing ivy-clad building is situated on the banks of the River Coln, at the point where it crosses the Roman Fosseway. The Bridge Bar dates from the 15th century and displays a wealth of beams, stone and sturdy furniture. There is a delightful riverside garden with a lake. Children are allowed in the Bridge Bar and restaurant only. Well appointed guest bedrooms are available.

On draught: Wadworth 6X, Marston's Pedigree, Hook Norton Best Bitter, Guinness, Beck's, Woodpecker and Dry Blackthorn ciders.

Food: quality bar food includes sandwiches (from £2.20), home-made soup (£1.95), steamed Brixham mussels (£3.95), crevette salad with lime vinaigrette (£4.25) and main dishes like red bream fillet with basil and tomato dressing. Sunday roasts (£7.50).

Times: 12-2pm and 7-9pm, (9.30pm in restaurant on Fri & Sat). Telephone: 0285 720721.

Chedworth

This is a large scattered village on the steep hillsides bordering the Coln Valley. Fine old cottages radiate from the church, which houses a beautifully carved stone pulpit. Above the village, at Denfurlong, there is a farm trail.

On leaving the pub locate the footpath alongside the inn, then cross the road to pass through an iron gate and proceed due west through a sloping pasture, with the river away to your left. Beyond a wooden gate, look out for a stile and bridge on your left and cross the river. Bear right and follow the path into Lower Chedworth, where you turn left along the road through the village, until reaching a grassy path on your right at a house called Saffron Hill. Turn left beyond the stile and stay above the stream, following the path through several pastures to emerge into Chedworth by a pub called the Seven Tuns, from where the church can be seen.

ℬIBURY ~to~ 𝒞OLN ST ALDWYNS

**APPROXIMATELY
6 MILES**

*An easy-going walk
across open farmland
and through riverside
parkland within the
delightful Coln
Valley. Both villages
are rich in
architectural history.*

Parking
OS Map 163 Ref SP1106.
Bibury village car park.

New Inn
Coln St Aldwyns, near
Cirencester - 2 miles north of
Fairford.

FURTHER EXPLORATION

Bibury
The village itself centres on
some fine old cottages round a
square on the north-west side
of the church. There is much to
see, such as St Mary's Church
which is rich in Saxon work

ocate Arlington Row (NT), situated between
Bibury church and the hamlet of Arlington,
cross the three-arch stone bridge and pass Rack Isle
and the fine row of 17th-century weavers cottages to
join the footpath which lies beyond the cottages up a
steep flight of steps. At the top go straight on, then
bear right and proceed in a southerly direction to a
metal gate and a waymarker. Turn left onto a firm
bridleway and follow it for 1½ miles through farmland
to a lane. Turn left, pass Coneygar Lodge, then in a few
yards turn left again to rejoin the footpath, which
crosses lush pasture towards a steel gate. Disregard the
stile on the left and continue straight on in front of a
pair of cottages, then head across a field towards the
elm and beech trees. Shortly, descend across grassland
towards the river, go through a gate beside Yew Tree
Lodge and turn left along the lane into Coln St
Aldwyns. Where the lane bears left away from the
river, the New Inn is on the right.

❧*New Inn* (Free House)❧

A fine ivy-clad 16th-century coaching inn offering a
warm welcome within its cosy and attractively
decorated bars. Rug-strewn floors, low beams, a stone
fireplace with log fire and a good mix of sturdy
furniture create a relaxed and homely atmosphere in
which to enjoy a hearty lunch. A raised terrace with
tables and chairs is ideal for fine weather lunching.
Children are welcome inside away from the bar.
Overnight accommodation available.

On draught: Hook Norton Best Bitter, Flowers IPA,
Wadworth 6X, Boddingtons, Murphy's, Stella Artois,
Heineken, Strongbow cider.
Food: the frequently changing menu features filled
rolls (£2.50), soup (£2.25), ploughman's (£4.34), club

sandwich with bacon and egg (£4.45), grilled mackerel
with dill butter (£5.50), half-dozen oysters (£7.50).
Puddings (£2.75). There is also a restaurant.
Times: 12-2.30pm and 6.30-9.30pm (Sun 7pm).
Telephone: 0285 750651.

From the inn turn left and retrace your steps back
to Yew Tree Lodge, then at the footpath
fingerpost take the lower waymarked path beside the
River Coln. This peaceful stretch of the walk is easy
and level across grassland and affords good views of
the river and a chance to observe the wildlife in the
valley. At a dry-stone wall climb a stone stile and pass
to the left of a copse used as a game bird enclosure
(take care in the shooting season), then bear right to
follow a track towards Bibury Court (Hotel) and a mill
beside the river. With the splendid hotel to your left,
walk up to the B-road and turn left to follow the road
past the church back into the village to your car.

and displays a fine collection
of sheep corbels, a tribute to
the former importance of wool
in village life. At the Trout
Farm visitors can catch their
own fish. Nearby is 17th-
century Arlington Mill which
houses a folk museum.

ᶓDGEWORTH ~to~ SAPPERTON

APPROXIMATELY 5 MILES

This walk explores the quietest and most hidden part of the Cotswolds and enjoys beautiful wooded views. It involves a couple of steep climbs and it can be very muddy underfoot.

Start of Walk

OS Map 163 Ref SO9405. In Edgeworth village

From the top of the road leading to the church, follow either the lane or the footpath to the church, which has Saxon and Norman origins and is well worth a visit. Keep to the lane to the end of the village, then cross the stone stile and follow the yellow arrow directing you straight ahead up a grassy slope to a wooden stile. Proceed across the field beyond, aiming for the gate located to the left of a stone house. Go over a double stile, a road and a further stile into pasture, then head towards the stile visible in the distance across the field. Climb over it, then keep close to the hedge on your left to cross a hidden stile into the next field. Traverse this pasture to a gate, then proceed downhill towards a house and climb the flight of steps to its left. From here your path is not waymarked as it follows the edge of a large pasture between woodland, eventually reaching a wooden gate. Keep straight on to descend a steep tussocky hill to a lane, then turn right to find the Daneway Inn.

☙*Daneway Inn (Free House)*☙

This busy and friendly pub was built in 1784 for the 'bargees' and 'leggers' who worked the long Sapperton Canal Tunnel until the Great Western Railway was built in 1911. It is now a popular refreshment spot and retains its traditional music-free atmosphere within its three rooms, one of which is a no-smoking family room with toys. The lounge bar is dominated by a magnificent carved fireplace. There is a large sloping flower garden with benches and good views across the Frome Valley.

On draught: Archers Best Bitter, Daneway Bitter, Bass, Wadworth 6X, guest ale, Guinness, Stella Artois, Castlemaine XXXX, Bland's Blackjack cider.
Food: good bar snacks include filled rolls (90p), filled jacket potatoes (£2.30), ploughman's (£2.50), chilli and salad (£3.60), vegetarian lasagne (£3.60) and hot apple pie (£1.20).
Times 12-2pm and 7-9.30pm (Sun 12-1.30pm and 7-9pm). Telephone: 0285 760297.

On leaving the pub follow the towpath of the now derelict Thames and Severn Canal, waymarked towards Sapperton, eventually crossing over the mouth of the canal tunnel to a stile. Climb the stile, go up the field towards the spire of Sapperton church and soon enter the churchyard. From the church, proceed down a grassy slope with a striking topiary hedge to your right, then bear right to a lane. Turn left, then almost immediately turn left again onto an arrowed path, which climbs steeply through woodland on what can be a muddy path. In spring an abundance of wild flowers line your route as you head uphill, keeping left at a fork to reach the top. Head across pasture to a track and pass through a wooden gate to follow a level grassy path beside a drystone wall, all the way back to the stone stile you crossed on your outward route. Descend into Edgeworth, retracing your steps back to your car.

Daneway Inn
Sapperton, near Cirencester. Off A419, 5 miles west of Cirencester.

FURTHER EXPLORATION

St Kenelm's Church, Sapperton
The church mainly belongs to the 14th century, although the Atkyns family of nearby Pinbury Park renovated it around 1730. Sir Robert Atkyns whose monument adorns the south transept, was the author of 'The Ancient and Present State of Gloucestershire', a famous historical treatise.

Miserden Park Gardens, Miserden
Lovely garden overlooking Golden Valley and open regularly in aid of the National Gardens scheme. For opening times consult their handbook.

*C*HIPPING CAMPDEN ~to~ *E*BRINGTON

**APPROXIMATELY
5½ MILES**

*A gently undulating
walk across farmland,
starting from the most
beautiful and historic
small market town in
the Cotswolds.*

Parking
OS Map 151 Ref SP1539 Public
car park in the town.

Ebrington Arms
Ebrington, near Chipping
Campden. Signposted from
B4035 east of Chipping
Campden.

*W*alk to the junction of Church Street and
Station Road on the north side of the church
and locate the 'Heart of England Way', which is
arrowed through the front garden of Forge Cottage
and then skirts the school into open farmland. Head
downhill, ignore the footpath to the left, bear left at the
bottom to a waymarked stile then climb a grassy slope
to a gate to the right of a farmhouse. Bear right (blue
arrow) across pasture and aim to be above the trees,
then descend the next field to a gate and turn left to
follow the stream for quarter of a mile before crossing
it via a plank bridge. Continue until you reach the next
plank bridge, turn right and leave the stream to climb
uphill beside a drainage ditch, along the edge of a field,
towards a cluster of black barns visible ahead and
reach a road. Cross over, pass through a gate into
pasture and head for the far steel gate, then bear right
(yellow arrow) over the next field to a gate and cross a
road. Beyond an arrowed gate, head towards apple

trees to a stile, then aim for the four hawthorn trees, which indicate the beginning of the track into Ebrington. Turn left in the village for the pub.

Ebrington Arms (Free House)

A delightfully unspoilt 16th-century village pub boasting a wealth of exposed low beams, two stone inglenook fireplaces - the one in the dining room is a particularly fine example - and sturdy traditional furnishings in its music-free bar. Children are welcome inside, guest rooms are available for overnight accommodation and outside there is a sheltered terrace with picnic tables.

On draught: Hook Norton Best Bitter, Donnington SBA, Bass, guest ale, Carling Black Label, Bulmers cider.

Food: is simple but good and includes sandwiches (from £1.75), ploughman's (£3.25), home-made steak and kidney pie and chicken, ham and tarragon pie (both £5.45), sirloin steak (£8.50) and omelettes (£3.85).

Times: 12-2pm and 7-9.30pm, except Sun evening.
Telephone: 038678 223

From the pub turn left, then take the road which leads behind the pub and shortly turn right into the driveway to Ebrington Fruit Farm. Walk through the orchard, eventually reaching a stile, then follow the yellow arrow across two fields, via a waymarked gate, to a stile/bridge. Bear diagonally left across lush pasture to a bridge and continue to the railway. Cross the track, bear half-right to a stile, then turn right for a little way along the main road, to where a footpath sign directs you left. After about 200 yards turn right between the crops, turning left then right at the end to a stile. Keep ahead towards the next stile, then bear right - or follow the edge of the field - uphill towards Chipping Campden. As your path descends across grassland, aim 50 yards to the left of the ruined stone arch and enter the town to get back to your car.

FURTHER EXPLORATION

Chipping Campden
'The most beautiful village street now left in the island' is how the historian G.M. Trevelyan described the heart of this fine market town. Wide and curved in the middle it narrows at each end in order (in former times) to contain the sheep on market days. It remains a lovely unbroken terrace of buildings with mullioned windows, steeply pitched gables and tall chimneys, dating from the 14th century. The Church of St James is the most magnificent of the Cotswold wool churches and one of oldest buildings - Woolstaplers Hall - houses the town museum.

Hidcote Manor
(2 miles north)
These formal and informal gardens, laid out by Major Lawrence Johnstone over 40 years, contain many rare trees, shrubs and plants of all kinds. They now belong to the National Trust. Telephone : 0386 438333.

*U*PPER HEYFORD
~to~*S*TEEPLE ASTON

APPROXIMATELY 5 MILES

A fairly level and easy walk through the Cherwell Valley and beside the Oxford Canal. The peace of the valley is, unfortunately, often shattered by passing jets from the nearby air base.

*W*alk down to the bottom of Mill Lane to the Oxford Canal and cross the bridge, then turn right to head north along the canal towpath. Pass under the railway, then on reaching a farmhouse, turn left through a gate and turn left again to follow a well marked path, until it reaches a large grassy field. Head diagonally left to a stile located close to an oak tree, then proceed straight on towards a single gate and cross a small stream. Keep to the right-hand edge of a field to where a gap presents itself into the next field. Either head diagonally uphill across it, or if the field is under cultivation, follow its edge round towards the village, to where the path emerges onto the road by Middle Aston House. Turn left, and remain on the road

for half-a-mile, turning right at the church to walk through the village to a road junction and the Red Lion.

⊖*Red Lion* (Free House)⊖

A friendly and civilised 300-year-old hostelry with a comfortably furnished beamed bar and separate dining room. Relax in the bar with a range of daily papers or take a good pint of ale out onto the sheltered flower-filled front terrace - a splendid spot in the summer. Children are not permitted inside.

On draught: Hook Norton Best Bitter, Wadworth 6X, Carlsberg.
Food: Good bar snacks are available lunchtimes only and may feature rare roast beef sandwiches, ploughman's (£3.20), smoked salmon roll for £2.30 and a home-made hot-pot in winter. More creative food is on offer in the evenings in the restaurant, where advance booking is necessary.
Times: 12-2pm and restaurant meals 7.30-9.15pm, except Sun and Mon. Telephone: 0869 40225.

*F*rom the pub turn left and follow the road until it gives way to a track, just beyond a small wood on your left. Proceed across a field on a defined path to a stile, then bear right to follow the stream before heading uphill between fields and woods to another stile. Go over the railway bridge, then bear half-right, heading downhill towards a stile, then left across a pasture between the river and some saplings to reach a mill. Cross the bridge, bear left and pass to the right of a gate to follow the path between the River Cherwell and the Oxford Canal, passing a 14th century tithe barn on your way back to Upper Heyford.

Start of Walk
OS Map 164 Ref SP4926. In Mill Lane.

Red Lion
South Street, Steeple Aston. Off A4260, 4 miles south of Deddington.

FURTHER EXPLORATION

Rousham House (2 miles south)
Here in peaceful seclusion, is a manorial village with wayside houses, a church and the great Rousham House. The house built in 1635 was used as a Royalist stronghold during the Civil War and enlarged in 1738 by William Kent who also surrounded it by a man-made landscape including classical temples, cascades and statues in 30 wooded acres within a bend of the River Cherwell. Garden open daily all year; house Apr- Sep, Wed, Sun and BH Mon. Telephone: 0869 47110

ƑINSTOCK ~to~ ℭHARLBURY

Parking
OS Map 164 Ref SP3616. In
the upper part of Finstock High
Street.

Bell
Shore Street, Charlbury -
B4022 between Witney and
Chipping Norton.

FURTHER EXPLORATION

Charlbury
The village overlooks the
Evenlode Valley towards
Wychwood Forest, a medieval
hunting ground that once
covered much of West
Oxfordshire. It is a compact
village with many narrow
streets of 18th-century
buildings. The Church of St
Mary the Virgin dates from
medieval times, and has a 700-
year old stairway and some
fine stained glass.

ind the Plough Inn on the southern side of the
village and follow the wide bridleway opposite
called Dark Lane. Shortly, fork left to cross two stiles
and a meadow to reach the banks of the River
Evenlode. Turn right along the bank - can be muddy -
then on reaching the railway bridge, go up the
embankment to cross the river and the non-electric
railway line before dropping down the embankment
on the other side into pasture. Cross the field to a stile
and enter Fawler. At Corner Cottage turn left along the
road, then turn right to join a concrete track, signed
towards Manor Farm Dairy. This soon gives way to a
wide hedged track, which becomes walled to your left.
At the end of the wall turn left to follow a delightful
woodland path - Oxfordshire Way - eventually
reaching a lane. Turn right, walk uphill for a little way,
then take the waymarked path left, following it to a
stile. Turn right down a lane to a busy village road,
cross over and head down Danes Hill, turning left then
right into the village centre. Turn left into Church
Street for the Bell.

urn left from the inn and follow the road
downhill for half a mile to where a waymarked
footpath directs you right towards Cranbury Park. Just
before the park gates turn left onto a well defined path
through the deer park, which shortly joins with an oak-
lined tarmac driveway to the busy B4022. Turn left,
then almost immediately right onto a concrete road
leading to a sewerage plant. Bear right behind the
plant to follow the path around the perimeter of a field
(may be under crop) to enter Finstock, close to the
village store. Turn left along the village street to retrace
your steps back to your car.

❧*Bell Hotel* (Free House)❧

This 17th-century coaching inn has a relaxing traditional bar complete with flagstone floor, oak furniture and log fire. Sporting guns, fly-fishing rods and prints adorn the walls. A larger, comfortably furnished, adjoining room welcomes children and there is also a garden. The inn has 15 bedrooms.

On draught: Hook Norton Best Bitter, Wadworth 6X, McEwan, Beck's lager.

Food: good quality bar snacks range from toasted sandwiches at £1.90 and an authentic selection of Spanish tapas dishes at £3.75 each, to a sirloin steak with pepper sauce for £6.75. The restaurant offers a 3-course Sunday lunch and the weekday table d'hôte is £12.50.

Times: 12-2.30pm, 6.30-8pm. Telephone: 0608 810278.

Blenheim Palace Woodstock

This grandiose mansion in extensive parkland was built by Sir John Vanbrugh for John Churchill, the 1st Duke of Marlborough after he had been awarded the Royal Manor of Woodstock after his victory over the French at Blenheim in 1704. One of its main attractions today is the room where Sir Winston Churchill was born in 1874. Telephone: 0993 811325 & 811091.

Abbots Morton ~to~ Inkberrow

**APPROXIMATELY
4¾ MILES**

*A gentle stroll
through rolling
Worcestershire
farming countryside.*

Start of Walk
OS Map 150 Ref SP0254.
Abbots Morton village hall, 50
yards from the church.

Old Bull
The Green, Inkberrow,
Worcester. Five miles west of
Alcester, off A422.

FURTHER EXPLORATION

Abbots Morton
Hidden away among a web of
lanes this splendid village is an
assemblage of black-and-white
cottages and houses of every
shape and design and has
often been described as the
most perfect village in the
country. Its lovely 14th-century
church stands surrounded by
trees on a small mound
overlooking the village, while
on the green stands a thatched
letterbox.

Head downhill, past the Post Office and through the attractive village. Turn left at the second waymarked footpath, pass in front of a bungalow, then bear left along the garden fence, straight across a field and turn right alongside the hedge, going through two fields to a join bridleway. Turn left, then at a left-hand bend, keep ahead through a gate and then keep right-handed through two fields onto a short track to a road. Bear left past cottages, then turn right onto a track and shortly bear left round a wood to a wooden bridge over a stream. Keep left round the field edge to the opposite corner by two big oak trees and turn left onto a bridleway. On reaching a road, turn right, pass Leach Farm and soon take the waymarked footpath left. Follow the left-hand hedge, and after 100 yards, do not go straight ahead, but bear slightly right along the hedge to pass a wooden gate on the left. Keep to the right-hand hedge, then turn right over a stile onto a track, just before a brick barn. Join a road, proceed uphill into Inkberrow, passing the church on your way to the pub.

☙ *Old Bull* (Free House) ☙

For over 40 years this ancient half-timbered hostelry has been the model for the 'Bull' at Ambridge in BBC radio's longest running soap opera, 'The Archers'. A pub since 1750, it oozes character and features huge inglenooks, stone flagged floors, oak beams and trusses. Various 'Archers' memorabilia abound. Its friendly atmosphere and lovely garden give it all the classic pub attributes. Children are welcome.

On draught: Wadworth 6X, Boddingtons Bitter, Flowers IPA, Banks Mild, Murphy's, Heineken, Dry Blackthorn cider and a good selection of wines.
Food: a wide range of wholesome bar meals includes soup (£1.95), lasagne (£3.75), ploughman's (£3.65), chicken fillet in cider, liver and onions, sandwiches

(from £1.75) and salads (£3.65). Puddings include apple
and rhubarb pie (£1.60).

Times: 12-2pm and 6.30-8.30pm (no food Sun
evenings). Telephone: 0386 792428.

---

rom the pub turn left, then at a junction go left
again, shortly to bear left into Pepper Street. At a
T-junction, turn left and take the footpath in the corner
of the road. Follow the left-hand edge of a field,
alongside a stream, and after 100 yards cross a stile
beside a large ash tree. Follow the left-hand hedgerow,
bearing right to a stile in the field corner. Go straight
across the next field, or follow the right-hand hedge if
it is in crop, into another field, then keep to the right-
hand hedge to a metal stile. Pass through a small
thicket, then follow the left-hand hedge of a field down
to a stile. Descend between trees to a bridge over a
stream into a field, then keep left-handed to a
waymarked gateway. Follow the track past a farm to a
gate and a road. Turn left to return to Abbots Morton.

Ragley Hall, Alcester
A stately Jacobean mansion
set in 400 acres of parkland
and gardens. The showpiece of
the house is the Great Hall
which contains some of the
finest Baroque plasterwork in
England, designed by James
Gibbs. Playground, maze and
woodland walks. Open: Etr to
Sep. Telephone: 0789 726090.

$\mathcal{H}$OARWITHY ~to~ $\mathcal{S}$ELLACK

$\mathcal{G}$o downhill, turn left, signposted Little Dewchurch, then at a fork keep right and cross the River Wye. Take the waymarked footpath right, following it between high hedges to a lane. Continue straight ahead and shortly pass the Church of St John the Baptist at Kings Caple. At a crossroads turn right downhill to a sharp bend, then bear right onto a footpath down to and across Sellack Boat, (suspension bridge) over the Wye. Go directly across the field and climb a stile onto a hard track beside St Tysilio Church. Turn right, continue past Caradoc Hall and the adjoining farm, to a crossroads. Turn left downhill and you will come to the pub on your right.

$\mathcal{L}$eave the inn, turn left, then immediately right opposite the road to Upper Grove Common, onto an arrowed footpath over a stile. Go across a small field to a stile, then down a large field to climb another stile into a wood. Go through the trees on a waymarked path to a stile and road. Turn left, pass Sellack church and return to Sellack Boat. Do not cross the bridge; instead, turn left along the riverside path, then on nearing a white cottage, bear left to join a road via a stile. Turn right past Sheppon Hill Cottage, remaining on the road for 500 yards to a waymarked stile on the left. Pass through two gates and immediately bear left, uphill to a tree and hedge on your right. Follow the hedge round to the left to cross a stile, then bear right-handed round the field edge to an arrowed stile and shortly join a track. Follow the track down to a road, turn left, then take a signed footpath on the right and bear left across a field to a stile. Maintain direction across three fields and stiles to reach some steps up to a road beside a toll house on the bridge. Turn left back into Hoarwithy.

☞*Lough Pool Inn* (Free House)☜

A handsome, half-timbered, 16th-century pub nestling beside a quiet lane deep in the countryside. Inside, a flagged floor, open fires, rustically furnished nooks and crannies and an abundance of dried flowers, sporting prints and farming bric-a-brac characterise this traditional and welcoming pub. Children are welcome in the snug bar and there is plenty of outdoor seating on the front lawn. Dogs are not allowed.

On draught: Bass, Wye Valley Hereford Supreme, Stones Best Bitter, Guinness, Carling Black Label, Stowford Press cider, good choice of malt whiskies.
Food: an interesting menu includes farmhouse pâté (£2.75), home-made soup (£1.90), ploughman's (£3.75), steaks (from £7.50), whole grilled John Dory, grilled shark steak (both £7.50) and a range of vegetarian dishes (from £5.75). Puddings (£2.50).
Times: 12-1.30pm, 7-9.30pm. Telephone: 098987 236.

Modiford
A beautiful, partly 14th-century bridge spans the River Lugg and among the attractive buildings in the little village are the Georgian Rectory and a Palladian mansion, Sufton Court (open occasionally) with a fine, landscaped park.

ᴅILWYN ~to~ ᴡEOBLEY

*W*ith the green on your right, follow the road gently uphill out of the village, bearing right, signed Weobley Marsh. Shortly, after passing a farm on your left, take the waymarked bridleway ahead. Keep left-handed along the edge of a wood to a gate, and head straight across the next field, through a metal gate, across an earthen bridge over a stream and along a farm track past farm buildings. Walk alongside a hedge to your left, towards a church with a spire, pass through three gates and cross a track to a stile. Proceed on a footpath to a road at the end of a cul de sac. Turn right and wend your way on the footpath through houses to join the main village road. Turn right for the Old Salutation.

ᴥ*Old Salutation Inn* (Free House)ᴥ

Dating back some 500 years, this fine, timbered inn commands a splendid position at the top end of a picture-book, black-and-white village. A civilised air pervades the comfortably furnished lounge bar with its log fire and exposed beams and the attractive adjoining restaurant. There is also a separate public bar with games, and five guest bedrooms. Children are welcome in the lower lounge, but no dogs are allowed inside.

On draught: Hook Norton Best Bitter, Boddingtons Bitter, Bass, Marston's Pedigree, Guinness, Newquay Steam Pils, Heineken, Stella Artois, Westons Old Rosie cider.

Food: bar meals include steak and Guinness pie (£5.60), chicken and basil fusili (£4.95), Indonesian stir-fry (£5.50), venison sausages with redcurrant and onion gravy (£5.50). There are also a set 3-course Sunday lunch and a separate restaurant menu.

Times: 12-2pm and 7-9.30pm (9pm in restaurant).. Telephone: 0544 318443.

———◆◆◆◆———

*W*alk down the main street, past the bowling green and the church to a sharp bend. Bear right, pass through the second gate left and follow the left-hand edge of a field to a double stile and footbridge in the bottom corner. Beyond, turn right along the hedge to a gate, then along the left-hand hedge and pass through another gate. With trees on your left, continue round the field edge for 300 yards, then make your way into the corner of the next field by some trees. Keep close to trees and a ditch to a double stile and bridge over a stream on your left. Turn left along the hedge to the top of the field to a gate and a road. Turn right, then left, at a junction, signed Haven. After 500 yards, turn right up a high-hedged lane, then at a T-junction turn right and continue to a waymarked footpath on your right. Go through a gate and straight across a field to a stile in the far corner. Turn left, go through a gate, across two stiles, then bear half-left downhill across a field to a gate onto a road. Turn left, then almost immediately right, to take an arrowed path right over a stile and then left down a field to a gate. Continue to a road, turn right and return to the village and your starting point.

Dilwyn

An attractive village with its fair share of black-and-white timbered houses around a diminutive green. Of interest is the impressive medieval and stone-built Church of St Mary, which has a spire mounted on a Norman tower, two medieval angels in glass and notable 15th-century screenwork. Luntley Court (not open) is one of the finest timber-framed buildings with a dovecote like a doll's house, dated 1673, opposite.

Weobley

Perhaps the most attractive village in an area famed for its 'black-and-white' settlements. Several cottages date back to the 14th century, as does the parish church with its lofty spire and interesting monuments. Earthworks survive from the former castle. South west of the village is The Ley, an eight-gabled, timbered farmhouse built in 1589.

$\mathscr{B}$RILLEY ~to~ $\mathscr{W}$HITNEY-ON-WYE

**APPROXIMATELY
5¾ MILES**

*An undulating walk
across open farmland,
close to the Welsh
border with fine views
over the Wye Valley
towards the Black
Mountains.*

Start of Walk
OS Map 148 Ref SO2649. Car
park outside St Mary's Church
in Brilley.

Rhydspence Inn
Whitney-on-Wye. Four miles
north-east of Hay-on-Wye, off
A438 Hereford to Brecon road.

FURTHER EXPLORATION

**Cwmmau Farmhouse,
Brilley**
An early 17th-century timber-
framed and stone-tiled
farmhouse. (National Trust).
Telephone: 0497 831251.

From the car park turn left and take the footpath on the left, just beyond Old Forge Cottage. Pass through a gate, keep to the left-hand hedge through two gates, then bear half-right across a field to a stile into a wood. Leave the wood via a stile, head half-right up a field to a stile by a water trough. Go half-left to cross two more stiles, then diagonally right across a field to another stile. Turn left down into a hollow to a stile and road. Turn left, then at a junction take the footpath on the right. Bear left across a field to a stile, proceed to a gate and turn right onto a track. Just before crossing a stream, take the hedged footpath on your left. Go through a gate, then in 200 yards turn left uphill to another gate and bear right along the hedge to a stile. At the next stile bear right and follow the right-hand hedge past farm buildings to another stile. Proceed to a gate, follow a track past a pond and where it bears right, keep straight onto a stile and road. Turn left, then right, opposite a farm to follow a footpath, left, down a field to a stile by a large oak. Maintain direction to another stile and turn right onto a road. Beyond a house, turn left onto a track, pass a farm and go through a gate, then follow the hedge on your right round the field to an old cottage. Pass through two gates to an old track through woods, then with a hedge on your left, go through two more gates to a track. Turn left, join a road, turn right and go downhill to reach the pub.

$\backsim$*Rhydspence Inn* (Free House)$\backsim$

An impressive black-and-white, 14th-century drovers' inn, located right on the Welsh border. The delightful timbered interior features heavy beams, old furniture, and real fires, with various bits of rural bric a brac decorating the walls. Well tended gardens and terraces have splendid views across the Wye Valley. The five ensuite bedrooms are full of character. Children are welcome, but not dogs.

On draught: Robinsons Best Bitter, Bass, Hook Norton Bitter, Carling Black Label, Dunkerton cider.

Food: the selection may include soup (£2.65), lasagne (£5.50), venison burger (£4.95), chicken tikka masala (£5.95), ploughman's (£4.25), spinach and mozzarella crunch (£4.95) and Rhydspence pasty (£4.25). There is a separate restaurant menu and traditional 3-course Sunday lunch (£10.95).

Times: 11am-1.45pm and 7-9.45pm (Sun 12-1.30pm and 7-9.30pm). Telephone: 0497 831262.

Hay-on-Wye

A small market town, set above one of Britain's most enchanting rivers, the Wye, with the Black Mountains, at their steepest and grandest, looming near. Narrow streets winding through the old town are full of fascinating small shops, in particular second-hand book shops. A castle was built here in Norman times and destroyed by Owain Glyndwr in the 15th century, but a fine gateway, the keep and parts of the wall remain.

From the inn, take the road steeply uphill for 300 yards to a stile on the right. Bear left to another stile, enter a wood and follow a track past a farm to a stile and road. Proceed uphill to a junction by an old farm and join a hedged track. Take the footpath in front of Old Shop Cottage, cross a stream and a field to a gate, then proceed over the next field to a stile. Go through a wood, up steps to a gate, then turn left and go through another gate. Turn right, pass farm buildings to a gate, then continue ahead to a kissing gate into the churchyard and and the car park.

£ASTHOPE ~to~ WENLOCK EDGE

APPROXIMATELY 5 MILES

An enjoyable ramble through typical rolling farmland with fine views from Wenlock Edge, looking north-west towards Shrewsbury.

Start of Walk
OS Map 138 Ref SO5695.
Easthope Church.

*G*o into the churchyard to the main church doors. Proceed along the right-hand side of the hedgerow opposite, following the field edge to a gate. Cross a stream, pass through a small wood, then turn immediately right alongside a pond. Beyond two more small ponds, go through a wooden gate and a further gate on your right into a large field. Keep to the left-hand fence towards some farm buildings and pass another small pond. Do not enter the farm, but keep right with Shropshire Way signs along a fence, and proceed to a gate in the field corner. Join a rough track, then at a T-junction, turn left uphill to a main road. Cross over, bear right downhill on a hard track through woods, then in 200 yards bear right again onto a track through trees. On reaching a fork, keep right uphill on a narrower woodland track to a waymarked post and soon join a road. Turn left and continue for 250 yards to the pub.

⌕*Wenlock Edge Inn (Free House)*⌕

This old quarryman's cottage dates from 1700 and enjoys a splendid secluded location, high up on a scenic ridge. Family-run, there is a friendly and welcoming atmosphere within the two comfortably furnished bars and small, intimate dining room. Open fires, a flowery terrace filled with picnic benches and four ensuite letting bedrooms add to the charm of this inn. Children are welcome, but no under 10s in the restaurant after 8pm on Saturdays.

On draught: Websters Yorkshire Bitter, Robinsons Best Bitter, guest ale, Carlsberg, Stowford Press cider, wide choice of malt whiskies.

Food: good-value, home-cooked fare may include tomato and sweet red pepper soup (£1.95), Scottish pâté (£3.20), steak and kidney pie (£4.60), Cumberland pie (£4.90), rump steak (£8.50), prawn salad (£3.60). Puddings (£2.10) range from chocolate chimney to raspberry and apple crumble.

Times: 12- 2pm and 7-9pm. Closed Mon lunchtime, except Bank Hols. Telephone: 0746 36403.

From the pub turn right onto the road (do not miss the beautiful views from the Wenlock Edge viewpoint) and shortly, at the second entrance to Wenlock Edge, drop down left onto a track. Eventually rejoin the road and continue for some 500 yards to a junction at Presthope. Turn right downhill towards Bourton, then after 100 yards turn right onto a footpath, waymarked 'Shropshire Way' and the 'Ippikins Way'. Continue past a building on your left, pass through a gate, then bear left through another gate and proceed around the field edge to an arrowed gate on your left. Head uphill through trees, then follow the waymarkers through fields and farmland and along a track back to Easthope Church.

Wenlock Edge Inn
Hill Top, Wenlock Edge. On B4371 between Much Wenlock and Church Stretton.

FURTHER EXPLORATION

Wenlock Edge
A wooded limestone escarpment running from Craven Arms to Ironbridge. About 550 acres belong to the National Trust. It is famous for its geology, in particular the coral reef exposures that were laid down over 400 million years ago. Also of note is the limestone flora, including nine species of orchid.

Wilderhope Manor
(near Easthope).
Located in rural isolation with views down Corvedale, this limestone house dates from 1586 and remains unaltered. It belongs to the National Trust, who let it to the Youth Hostels Association. Open two afternoons between Apr and Sep. Telephone: 06943 363.

$\mathcal{L}$OWER DINCHOPE ~to~ $\mathcal{W}$ISTANSTOWE

**APPROXIMATELY
5½ MILES**

*A pleasant walk
through undulating
farmland.*

Start of Walk

OS Map 137 Ref SO4584. Park on the grass verge close to Lower Dinchope signpost, or, and only with permission from the owner, at Lower Dinchope Farm.

Plough Inn

Wistanstow, Craven Arms. Village signposted off A49 and A489 north of Craven Arms.

FURTHER EXPLORATION

Stokesay Castle, Stokesay

A well preserved 13th-century manor house in a romantic setting. Features include a fine gatehouse, the great hall and, reached by an outside staircase, a solar with 17th-century panelling. Open: Mar to Oct. Telephone: 0588 672544.

$\mathcal{F}$ollow the road signed Craven Arms, going down then uphill to a metal gate into a field on the right. Keep to the left-hand hedge to a stile, then head down through trees to a fence on your left and continue down and round to a waymarked stile on your left. Bear right along the hedge, climb a stile and continue beside the fence to a waymarked gate in the bottom of the field. Keep left to a gate in the opposite corner of the next field, then follow the hedge to a double stile and along a footpath through trees to a stile into a further field. Maintain direction across this field, passing close to a thicket on your left to a gate and stile on the left and join a track. Cross a gravel track with cottages on your right, then follow the left-hand edge of a field, keeping straight on to a stile into the next field. Cross to a small bridge, turn left and go across a larger bridge over a stream. Follow the left-hand hedge, climb a stile, cross a brook and go up the field to a stile onto the main road. Cross to follow a road into Wistantow. At a T-junction turn left for the pub.

⟿ *Plough Inn (Free House)* ⟿

This rough-stone building dates from 1774 and is the home to the Woods Brewery, whose beers are brewed in the adjacent building. A popular village local, it has been comfortably modernised inside over the years. There are three carpeted bars and the large lounge bar in particular has a good, welcoming atmosphere. Children are allowed in the games bar and dining area if eating. Outdoor seating and play area.

On draught: Woods Parish Bitter, Special Bitter, Wonderful and Strong, Murphy's, Heineken, Carling Black Label, Weston's cider, wines by the glass.
Food: home-made bar meals with separate menus for lunchtime, evenings and Sundays. Dishes may include duck breast and plum sauce (£6.95), local pigeon in red

wine and port (£5.75), rabbit in vermouth and cream
£4.75), chicken in cider pie (£4.75), halibut in wine and
cream (£7.50). Lunchtime snacks include sandwiches
from £1.50), pâté (£2.50), ploughman's (£3.50) and
steak and kidney pie (£4.75). Puddings (£1.75).
Times: 12-1.45pm and 7-9pm. No food Sun evening in
winter. Closed all day Mon, except Bank Hols.
Telephone: 0588 67251.

From the pub, turn right and pass through the
churchyard, leaving it via a kissing gate. Cross a
field to a waymarked stile, go over a small bridge and
cross the next field to a further stile. Continue ahead,
passing the middle of three oak trees, then at the field
edge, ignore the track ahead to a gate and instead turn
right along the hedge to cross a railway line via stiles.
Keep the hedge on your left and shortly cross a small
brook to a road. Cross and follow a metalled road to a
bridge over a stream beside a ford. Turn left, then after
100 yards turn right onto a hedged track. Proceed
uphill through a wooden gate, and shortly turn left
along a track. In 300 yards turn right onto a gravel
track, then at a T-junction with a road, turn right and
return to your starting point.

**Acton Scott Historic
Working Farm, Acton
Scott**

An old estate farm giving a
vivid introduction to traditional
rural life, with all work on the
farm done by hand or horse
power. There are daily craft
demonstrations and displays of
old equipment and machinery.
A farm cottage gives a glimpse
of domestic life at the turn of
the century. Open: Apr to Oct.
Telephone: 0694 781306 and
781307.

STIPERSTONES ~to~ BRIDGES

**APPROXIMATELY
6 MILES**

*A splendid walk
through open
Shropshire hill
country with fine
views of the
Stiperstones and the
Long Mynd.*

Start of Walk
OS Map 137 Ref SO3797.
Large National Nature Reserve
car park directly below the
Stiperstones.

Horseshoe Inn
Bridges, near Church Stretton.
North-west of Church Stretton
and A49, over the Long Mynd

FURTHER EXPLORATION

**Carding Mill Valley and
Long Mynd, Church
Stretton**
The National Trust owns 5,850
acres of moorland, extending 4
miles across the Long Mynd.
Carding Mill Valley has a shop,
cafe and Information Centre in
the Chalet Pavilion.
Magnificent views across
Shropshire and the Cheshire
Plain from the top of the Long
Mynd. Chalet Pavilion open:
Apr to Sep. Telephone: 0694
722631.

Go through the gate at the end of the car park, with the Stiperstones on your left, and walk along a track through two gates to join another track waymarked to the right down to Hollies Farm. Follow a road to a T-junction, turn left and after 100 yards go right through a metal gate onto a track. Go through another gate, bear right and keep on the track to a fence on the right. Head uphill, with the fence on your left, go round a fenced-off rectangle and cross a stile in the fence. Bear right to a clump of trees and join a track via a metal gate. Turn left, pass a farm, and at a T-junction, turn right and follow the road to the pub.

$\backsim$*Horseshoe Inn* (Free House)$\backsim$

Nestling in unspoilt countryside below the Long Mynd and beside a tumbling brook, this attractive inn boasts a wealth of beams, a stone-flagged bar and a pleasant carpeted lounge where children are welcome. Dogs on leads may be allowed in the public bar and there is a patio/terrace for outdoor drinking.

On draught: Marston's Pedigree, Worthington Best Bitter, Adnams Southwold Bitter, Eldridge Pope Blackdown Porter, guest ale, Murphy's, Tennant Pilsner, Bitburger Pils.
Food: a good selection of hearty snacks, such as home-made soup (£1.35), vegetable lasagne with garlic bread (£2.40), Shropshire Blue ploughman's (£2.25) and sandwiches (from £1).
Times: 12-2pm only.Closed Mon lunchtime.
Telephone: 058861 260.

On leaving the inn, cross a small footbridge over the stream, then a stile and bear half-left across a field to a metal gate and road. Turn left, then after 300

yards turn right onto a waymarked footpath through a
metal gate. Head diagonally left across a field to a stile
by an oak tree and proceed ahead with a fence to your
left to join a track. Cross a stream, pass through a gate
and turn right onto a road. Pass Kinnerton Farm, then
after 400 yards, turn right onto a track along the left-
hand side of the hill, aiming for a hedgerow and trees
on the skyline. Go through a gate and head across the
next field, passing to the right of a small building to a
further gate. Proceed uphill, close to a hedge and ditch
on your left, to cross a wire fence in the top corner of
the field. Continue uphill using the zig-zag path to the
brow of the hill. Ignore the stile directly ahead, instead
turn right along the ridge footpath. Eventually join a
road just below the car park

Stiperstones

This jagged ridge of quartzite
tors is steeped in myth and
legend. When the summit is
shrouded in mist, it is said that
the devil occupies his craggy
'chair'. The moorland is a
prime example of the
restricted range of plants
characteristic of extremely
exposed and acid conditions.

ℒEEBOTWOOD ~to~ 𝒫ICKLESCOTT

APPROXIMATELY 5½ MILES

A peaceful walk through rolling Shropshire farming countryside.

Parking
OS Map 137 Ref SO4490. Large layby on the left-hand side of the road 250 yards beyond St Mary's Church in Leebotwood.

Bottle and Glass Inn
Picklescott, Church Stretton. Village signposted off A49, north of Church Stretton.

*H*ead back towards Leebotwood, then in 20 yards, turn right and follow a road uphill to a waymarked footpath on the right. Cross a field to a stile, then bear left downhill to a small bridge over a stream. Cross two stiles, then keep right-handed alongside a fence to pass a white farmhouse on your left. Cross two stiles, a stream and another stile, then bear diagonally left uphill across a field to a gate in a hedge. Beyond this and a second gate on the left, head diagonally up a field to a gate onto a road. Turn left passing the church of St Michael, Woolstaston, then shortly turn right onto a track just before Pine Cottage. Cross a field, climb a stile, then bear left downhill to a gate. Turn right down to another gate, cross a stream, and ascend to a gate between two oak trees. Turn left, follow the hedge to a gate onto a track and turn left, soon to pass through a wooden gate to join a metalled track. Turn left then, on reaching a road, turn right for the pub.

⇔*Bottle and Glass Inn* (Free House)⇔

This delightful 17th-century country pub offers a warm welcome and a friendly atmosphere in front of the open inglenook fires, in the two beamed and neatly refurbished bars. A fine display of horse brasses and farming memorabilia decorate the bars. Children are welcome, but not dogs. Three en suite guest bedrooms are available. Outside are a patio and pleasant garden.

On draught: Bass, Worthington Best Bitter, Stones Best Bitter, Mitchells and Butlers Mild, good range of wines.
Food: an extensive range of food includes sandwiches (from £2), filled jacket potatoes (from £2), seafood platter (£3.50), roast beef platter (£4.95), rustler's grill (£8.95), Sunday lunch carvery (£7.75). Evening carvery (£12.95) and buffet menus by arrangement.
Times: 12-2pm and 7-9.30pm. Telephone: 0694 751345.

A t the crossroads outside the pub turn left to pass the post box and later Top House, before turning right on a road, signed 'Church only'. Take the waymarked bridleway, right, through a gate, follow the arrows across a field to another gate and keep on to a stream. Pass through a waymarked gate onto a track then, at a fork, bear left uphill, with a white cottage to your left. Beyond a wooden gate turn right along a road until you reach a left-hand bend and go through a gate on the right. Bear left, then after 100 yards, at a pair of gates, turn right following the hedge on your left to a wooden gate into a field. Proceed to a further gate on the right, then head downhill to a small bridge over a stream to Old Mill Farm. Follow the track, turn right to Yew Tree Farm, then at a left-hand bend turn right through a gate and immediately cross a double stile on your left. Keep the hedge on your left, cross a field to a gate onto a track and continue through two more gates onto a hard track. Turn left, come to a road and turn right, then right again at a T-junction back to your car.

Church Stretton
During the late 19th century the distict around the town became known as 'Little Switzerland' and Church Stretton developed into a popular inland resort. Red-brick and half-timbered Victorian villas mingle with older black-and-white buildings to create a pleasant character, complemented by the Church of St Lawrence, which dates back to the 12th century.

Leebotwood
Attractive half-timbered houses can be seen, notably the thatched Pound Inn which has the date 1650 on an outside beam and fine interior panelling. The church dates back to the 13th century. North-west of the church, on Castle Hill, is a 260ft-long mound that was probably an early Saxon fortification built over a prehistoric barrow.

STOW BEDON ~to~ THOMPSON

**APPROXIMATELY
5 MILES**

*An interesting walk
through a most
unusual area. Part of
the walk meanders
through pingoes -
shallow, swampy
ponds formed 200,000
years ago by under-
ground lenses of ice.
Dogs are not allowed
in the nature reserve.*

Parking

OS Map 144 Ref TL9679. Car
park on A1075 at the start of
Great Eastern Pingoe Trail, just
outside Stow Bedon.

Chequers

Griston Road, Thompson -
village off A1075 Thetford to
Watton road.

FURTHER EXPLORATION

Grimes Graves (7 miles
north-west of Thetford)
An area of hundreds of pits
dug by Neolithic people who
were mining for flint between
3000BC and 1900BC, this is the
largest group of prehistoric
flint mines in Britain. Open all
year. Telephone: 0842 810656.

From the car park, follow the Pingoe trail and keep
straight on where it forks between two largish
ponds. On reaching Butters Hall Lane turn left, keep on
past paddocks, cottages and a barn, then continue
diagonally across a field to a stile. Keep to the track
beside a stream across Thompson Carr (common land)
and eventually skirt Thompson Water. At a broad track
turn right and shortly join a metalled lane leading into
the village. At a large red barn on the left, take the
right-hand fork, then bear left-handed at the next fork.
Go over a crossroads and the pub is a short distance
along the road on the left.

↩*Chequers* (Free House)↪

This attractive long, low, thatched pub dating from the
16th century has retained its old low doors and
beamed ceilings throughout its three charming rooms.
Bygones adorn the walls and an inglenook fireplace
and a woodburner warm the bars in winter. Children
are welcome in the eating area. No dogs.
On draught: Adnams Bitter, Bass, Fuller's London
Pride, Worthington Best Bitter, Guinness, Carling Black
Label, Kingfisher Farm cider.
Food: an extensive menu includes pâté (£2.20), jacket
potatoes with fillings (from £2.25), steaks (from £7) and
steak and kidney pie (£3.50). Puddings (£1.75).
Times: 12-2pm and 6.30-10pm (Sun 12-1.30pm and 7-
10pm). Telephone: 0953 83360

On leaving the pub turn left into Griston Road
and follow this peaceful lane for about half a
mile. Continue a short distance past a waymarked path
on your right to join a grassy track (Drive Lane) on the
right and follow it between scrub with pingoes and
farmland to a road. Turn right, then next left into
Butters Hall Lane and shortly turn left again to rejoin
the track back through the pingoes to the car park.

SALTHOUSE HEATH

Walk along the road towards Cley or on the path through the woods, parallel to the road, if it is not too overgrown. At a road junction cross onto a waymarked path to Walsey Hills. Keep straight ahead, downhill towards the sea with superb views over the salt marshes. At a road turn left, then shortly turn right either to follow the track along the dyke through the nature reserve or alongside the reserve in the lee of the shingle bank to the beach. Turn left, walk along to the car park and head inland along the dyke and past the windmill to join the main road in Cley for the pub.

George & Dragon Hotel *(Free House)*

This seaside Victorian hotel is very popular with birdwatchers. On its second floor are a hide, a telescope and a large book of cuttings and notes on rare sightings on the nearby reserve. There is a good pubby atmosphere in the bars. Children are welcome, but not dogs at mealtimes.

On draught: Greene King IPA, Abbot Ale and Rayments Bitter, Murphy's, Carlsberg,
Food: an interesting menu features pan haggerty (£4.95), fish platter (£4.75), sandwiches (from £1.60), ploughman's (£3.50), local crab and shellfish.
Times: 12-2pm and 7-8.45pm. Telephone: 0263 740652.

Turn left from the pub, and left again by Whalebone Tearoom onto a narrow lane. Turn right at the end onto a road to the village hall, then left onto a track through abandoned allotments. Where it ends, turn right into Old Woman's Lane and follow it to the main road. Turn left, cross over and take the arrowed path right, uphill through a small wood, then downhill, across fields to a road to a quarry. Turn immediately left onto a track, head across fields to a junction with the Cley/Holt road. Go straight across and follow the lane back to Salthouse Heath.

APPROXIMATELY 6½ MILES

An easy level walk across heath and marshland on established paths, including the Peddars Way, with the opportunity to see some interesting birds, if you take your binoculars.

Parking
OS Map 133 Ref TG0742. Taylors Wood, Salthouse/Holt crossroads on Salthouse Heath.

George & Dragon Hotel
High Street, Cley-next-the-Sea. On A149 east of Blakeney.

FURTHER EXPLORATION

Shell Museum Glandford
Houses sea shells and curios collected by Sir Alfred Jodrell. Telephone: 0263 740081.

North Norfolk Railway, Sheringham
Steam railway with a collection of locomotives and rolling stock. Telephone: 0263 822045.

ℬECCLES ~to~ 𝒢ELDESTON

**APPROXIMATELY
6 MILES**

◆•◆•◆

*A pleasant, easy walk
along the banks of the
River Waveney, pass-
ing the attractive old
townscape of Beccles
and crossing lush
watermeadows,
marshes and
farmland.*

◆•◆•◆

*L*eaving the car park take the footbridge across
the backwater and follow the road towards the
town centre. At the first crossroads, with Ravensmere,
turn right over the bridge, then immediately left onto a
broad path through a boatyard. On reaching another
bridge, a yellow waymarker directs you onto a
beautiful riverside path. Continue for just over a mile,
then beyond a spinney at a T-junction, turn left
towards the river. The sign 'Locks Inn half a mile' is for
those arriving by boat. On reaching the junction of
river and canal, turn right along the canal bank, then
just before Geldeston village, pass under a bridge and
shortly follow sign for Wherry Inn straight ahead. At
the main road turn left, then at a crossroads, go left
again towards Ellingham. Beyond the entrance to a
caravan site turn left, waymarked Locks Inn, onto a
track over the marshes to the inn.

⮌Locks Inn *(Free House)*⮎

Built in 1563, the Locks retains an unspoilt bar with flagged floor, beamed ceiling, rough tiled-topped tables, gas lights, candles and open fires., but there are also new extensions. Popular with boating people, the pub stands in isolated marshland beside the River Waveney. Children and dogs are welcome inside and there are plenty of tables and chairs outside for pleasant summer drinking.

On draught: Woodforde's Nelson's Revenge, Wherry Bitter, Headcracker, Baldric and Nog, Scrumpy Jack and James White Suffolk cider.

Food: generous helpings of hearty home-cooked food are served, including soup (£1.65),'Doorstopper' sandwiches (from £1.10). Locks hotpot (£4.25), shepherd's cobbler (£4.15), macaroni cheese (£2.95), salads (from £3), burgers (from £2.30) and Locks special ploughman's (from £2.40). Puddings usually include fruit pie (£1.65) and bread pudding (85p). There is also a separate children's menu.

Times: 12-2.30pm and 7.30-10pm. The inn may be closed on weekday lunchtimes Jan to Etr, so it is advisable to check in advance. Telephone: 050845 414.

---

*O*n leaving the pub cross the river and its tributaries via three bridges, then head straight over the field (track is faint) to a stile and footpath. Turn left onto a clearly waymarked path and follow it through pleasant open country towards Beccles, visible in the distance. At the busy main road turn left for about quarter of a mile, then just beyond Roose Hall, turn left into Pudding Moor and follow this delightful, quiet lane, which passes between the houses lining the river bank and the cliff on which the town centre stands. There are some interesting side alleyways and paths to explore. Emerging at the old market, turn left along Northgate, back to the quayside and cross the footbridge back into the car park.

Parking
OS Map 134 Ref TN4290. Free car park near the quay and Tourist Information Office in Beccles.

Locks Inn
Geldeston, Beccles - off A143 3½ miles west of Beccles

FURTHER EXPLORATION

Otter Trust Bungay
Covering 20 acres on the banks of the River Waveney the Trust has a breeding programme designed to reintroduce young otters into the wild. As well as otters there is a collection of European waterfowl, walks and picnic areas.
Open Apr to Oct. Telephone: 0986 893470.

Beccles
Beccles Quay on the River Waveney is an ideal centre for exploring the network of local waterways. The Church of St Michael is the focal point of this pleasant country town. It has a detached bell-tower, a massive 14th-century structure rising to a height of 97ft, with a peal of ten bells. The town hall dates from 1726 and there are many fine Georgian houses.

$\mathcal{S}$HOTTISHAM ~to~ $\mathcal{R}$AMSHOLT

APPROXIMATELY 6½ MILES

An easy-going walk on established paths and bridleways through gently undulating countryside. A pleasant path follows the banks of the River Deben, the mud flats, salt marshes and meadows, home to many varieties of plants and animals.

Start of Walk
OS Map 169 Ref TM3244. Near the entrance to Shottisham church in Church Lane.

Ramsholt Arms
Dock Road, Ramsholt, Woodbridge. Off B1083 south-east of Woodbridge.

FURTHER EXPLORATION
Ramsholt
Once a busy little hamlet, with its quay filled with sailing barges bringing coal for the area and leaving with cargoes of crops. The church dates from the 13th century and is one of the few still without electricity.

$\mathcal{P}$roceed down Church Lane, turn left beside Tower Cottage to follow a footpath past allotments, then across a ditch and stile onto common land. Continue over two mini-bridges, then bear left-handed onto a path across a meadow towards a solitary red-brick building (Wood Hall Lodge). Cross the ditch and stile opposite the lodge, then follow the tarmac drive to pass to the left of Wood Hall Hotel. Keep left at a fork, then on reaching a junction turn left towards Pettistree Hall. Follow a wide track through the farm, remaining on the track round a right-hand bend and down to the river. Join a footpath along the river bank (can be difficult at high tide) and follow it to the pub which is situated on the river front.

$\backsim$*Ramsholt Arms (Free House)*$\backsim$

The Ramsholt Arms stands in a delightful isolated position among pine woods with magnificent views over the River Deben from the picture windows and paved terrace. A nautical theme dominates the simple, yet comfortably furnished bar, which is warmed by an open fire. Children are welcome in the dining area and overnight accommodation is available.

On draught: Adnams Bitter and Broadside, guest ales, Carlsberg and Export, Heineken.
Food: lunch and evening bar meals may include ploughman's (from £3.25), salads (from £4.95), cod and chips (£3.95), Dover Sole (£7.95), ham, egg and chips (£5.50), cold mixed fish platter (£7.50). Main evening menu features mussels in garlic butter (£2.95), steaks (from £8.75) escalope of veal (£7.25) with pavlova or spotted dick (£2.25) for pudding.
Times: (bar meals) 12-2pm and 7-9.30pm. Pub open 11am - 11pm Jul and Aug. Telephone: 0394 411229.

n leaving the pub, retrace your steps as far as the river and turn right. When you reach the edge of the pub grounds, turn right again onto a bridleway. Go through a gate, and follow the meandering path that takes you towards and to the right of the round-towered church. When you reach a junction of paths, proceed straight across, and then, ignoring the first path that you see on your right, turn right at a T-junction of paths and follow this clearly defined bridleway until you reach a road. Here turn left and when you come again to a T-junction, keep straight ahead to join a wide sandy track you will see running to the left of a house and follow it into Shottisham village. At the end of the track, if you continue straight on ahead, you will find yourself in Church Lane back at the starting point of the walk.

Woodbridge

Attractive houses of major historical interest surround the old market square round which this port has grown. Many date from the 16th century, and are centred on the superb Shire Hall, with its picturesque Dutch-style gables, which features work from the 16th to 19th centuries.

Woodbridge Tide Mill

Situated on the busy quayside, the mill looks towards the historic site of the Sutton Hoo Ship Burial. Machinery has been completely restored in this rare 18th-century survival and there are photographs and working drawings on display. Telephone: 0473 626618.

ƑRESTON ~to~ ƤIN MILL

*A gentle walk through
pasture and parkland,
close to the River
Orwell.*

Parking
OS Map 169 Ref TM1739.
Lay-by on the right-hand side
of B1456, just beyond the
Freston Boot.

Butt and Oyster
Pin Mill, Chelmondiston.
Signposted from B1456 south-
east of Ipswich.

FURTHER EXPLORATION

Flatford Mill Dedham
(southwest of Ipswich)
Once the home of the painter
John Constable, it now houses
a field-study centre. It is not
open to the public, but large
groups can arrange in advance
to be shown round. Next to the
mill, in Bridge Cottage, is a
visitor centre, information on
Constable, a tea room and a
shop. Both the mill and cottage
are owned by the National
Trust.

ake the waymarked footpath on the opposite side
of the road, then at a T-junction, turn right along
a track (becomes metalled) and follow it to where it
bends right. Keep straight ahead onto an unmarked
path between a hedge and field, cross over a lane
signed Woolverstone House and proceed through
woods to another road arrowed Woolverstone Marina.
Cross over, pass through an iron gate and head
towards the church with the hedge to your right, then
take the footpath waymarked River Orwell, which
points to the rear of the church. Just beyond the
church, at a gap in the hedge (signposted), take the left-
hand path through woodland following the marker on
your right in the clearing to a picket fence. Turn left,
then right onto the drive of the Royal Harwich Yacht
Club and walk towards the river, then take the
footpath arrowed right just before the road curves left.
The path immediately forks, and you take the lower
path, keeping left at each junction, eventually reaching
Pin Mill and the pub located on the river front.

rom the pub, walk uphill along the road, then
take the second footpath on the right just beyond
a car park. Climb a stile, head downhill to cross the
left-hand stile at the bottom of the hill, then walk
diagonally uphill across pasture to a gate and stile.
Proceed along a rough road to a T-junction, turn right,
then on reaching a right-hand bend, bear off left onto a
bridleway. Shortly cross a road, then at a second road,
follow the right-hand footpath sign along the country
road, turning left at a fork onto a farm track and
passing a house. Continue to a sharp left-hand bend,
then bear right onto a path, waymarked to Freston.
Keep to the edge of a field and across pasture to a road
leading to Woolverstone church. Facing the church,
bear left, keeping the hedge on your left, to an iron gate
and road. Cross over and retrace your steps back to
your car.

☙*Butt and Oyster* (Pubmaster)❧

Perched right on the edge of the River Orwell, this classic unspoilt pub is popular among the sailing and fishing fraternity. A rustic interior has old settles, tiled floors, a nautical theme and splendid views down the estuary from the waterside window seat. In suitable weather most of the clientele favour the outdoor terrace which also has superb river views. There is a family room.

On draught: Tolly Cobbold Bitter, Original and Mild, Tetley Bitter, Guinness, Carlsberg, Labatts, Stella Artois, Dry Blackthorn cider
Food: good home-made fare includes smoked chicken and mushroom pie (£4.50), ploughman's (from £2.50), seafood platter (£4.75), scampi (£4.25), tiger tail prawns in garlic butter (£5) and a range of sandwiches (from £1.10).
Times: (bar meals) 12-2pm and 7-10pm (9.30pm Sun). Pub open 11am-11pm May to Sep.
Telephone: 0473 780764.

Willy Lott's Cottage
A private house, not open to the public, this was one of Constable's most celebrated subjects and the home of one of his friends.

Ipswich
A predominantly Victorian town with little remaining of its medieval ancestry when it prospered on its cloth trade. Of interest is Christchurch Mansion, built on the site of an Augustinian priory in 1548 in a beautiful park and housing an art gallery - open all year. Telephone 0473 253246.

Ipswich Museum contains local geology and archaeology from prehistoric to medieval times - open all year. Telephone 0473 213761.

$\mathcal{P}$RESTON ST MARY ~to~ $\mathcal{L}$AVENHAM

**APPROXIMATELY
5½ MILES**

*An easy and pleasant
walk through farm-
land.*

Start of walk
OS Map 155 Ref TL9550. At
Preston St Mary church.

Angel
Market Place, Lavenham - on
A1141 between Hadleigh and
Bury St Edmunds

FURTHER EXPLORATION

Lavenham
One of the most outstandingly
beautiful villages in East
Anglia, hardly changed in
appearance since its heyday as
an important wool town in the
14th and 15th centuries. The
church carries a grand 141ft
tower and inside are a fine
Spring chapel of 1525 and
some good screenwork.

Lavenham Guildhall
Dates from the early 16th century and was the original meeting hall of the Guild of Corpus
Christi. A splendid example of
a close studded timber-framed
building. Telephone: 0787
247646.

*F*ollow the footpath opposite the church beside a concrete drive, at the end of which climb a stile and turn left to cross two fields littered with old vehicles. Turn left on reaching a road, then at a triangle junction take the waymarked footpath right, cross a bridge, go up some steps, and head uphill on a defined path through fields. At a farm track turn right, then left on reaching a road. In about 200yds turn right into Clay Lane, an established bridleway which leads across Clay Hill towards Lavenham. At the base of Clay Hill turn left, then take the second right along Barn Street for the pub.

✎*Angel* (Free House)✎

A delightful inn first licensed in 1420, the Angel overlooks the medieval market place and guildhall. The bars are cosy and relaxed with scrubbed pine and dark oak furniture, a huge inglenook fireplace and various china, paintings and teapots on display. Weekly events and live classical piano entertain. Picnic-style tables are set out to the front and there is more seating in the sheltered rear courtyard and garden. Children are welcome. Overnight accommodation is available.

On draught: Ruddles County, Courage Directors, Websters Yorkshire Bitter, Nethergate Bitter, Adnams Bitter, Guinness, Carlsberg, Holsten, Strongbow cider, good selection of wines and 17 malt whiskies.
Food: above average home-cooked dishes may include pea and mint soup (£2.25), warm chicken liver salad (£4.25), lamb in paprika and cream (£6.95), duck breast with blackcurrant sauce (£8.25), rabbit braised in cider and mustard (£8.25). Puddings (£2.45).
Times: 12-2pm and 7-9pm, restaurant 7-9.15 only. Telephone: 0787 247388.

On leaving the pub head downhill into Prentice Street. At the bottom of the hill, cross the road onto a waymarked footpath and cross the River Brett. Bear left on a well worn path, shortly to turn right at a junction of paths. Keep the ditch to your left, then at a hedge turn left, and follow the line of the hedge to a gap. Here, cross the ditch (there is no bridge) and follow the path between hedges and ditches to a private road. Cross this road, pass through the hedge and keep right, following the perimeter of the field, to a wide gap in the opposite corner. Go through this gap, keeping the hedge on your left, then shortly pass through an unmarked gap in the trees. Follow the path straight across a field, through another gap in the hedge and keep on, heading towards Preston St Mary. On reaching the lane you turn right to head back to the church and the starting point of the walk.

Lavenham Priory
This fine medieval timber-framed building was built for Benedictine monks in 1600. Well restored. Herb garden. Telephone: 0787 247417.

**Kentwell Hall
Long Melford**
Tudor mansion surrounded by a broad moat. Exhibition of Tudor-style costume, maze, walled garden, special events. Telephone: 0787 310207.

**Melford Hall
Long Melford**
Charming old red-brick Tudor house with panelled banquetting hall and Regency library. Telephone: 0787 880286.

ℰARLS COLNE ~to~ ℂHAPPEL

APPROXIMATELY 5¼MILES

A lovely walk across farmland and through woodland in the delightful Colne Valley, affording a variety of vistas.

Parking
OS Map 168 Ref TL8628. In Ley Road, near the river off the A604 at Earls Colne.

𝓌alk away from the A604 towards the open countryside, then at a sharp right-hand bend keep straight on onto a waymarked sandy track (Chalkney Trail). Go uphill into a clearing, pass through a gate on your left and enter woodland. At a junction keep ahead, then at a fork bear right (one red marker), remaining on this path to two gates and a road. Turn right and take the second footpath left, just before the top of the hill and Lambert's Farm. Climb uphill on a defined footpath, pass through a corrugated iron tunnel, then follow the well waymarked path (yellow markers) through an orchard eventually reaching a white house. Join the track/drive beside the house, walk on past another house, and keep left where a road joins from the right. Just before a solitary house on your right, take the arrowed footpath left, diagonally across a meadow towards the church spire to a stile in the bottom right-hand corner. Keep on to another stile beside farm buildings, turn right along a road, then turn left at Swan Lane for the pub.

⊙*Swan Inn (Free House)*⊙

Atmospheric and friendly, this 14th-century pub has a spacious low-beamed lounge bar, where the main feature is a large fireplace with a good winter fire. There is also a splendid sun-trap courtyard and a sheltered garden. Children welcome in the eating area.

On draught: Greene King IPA and Abbot Ale, Boddington's, Murphy's, Heineken, Stella Artois, Dry Blackthorn cider and several wines by the glass.
Food: a good selection of tasty bar food ranges from ploughman's (from £2.95) and sandwiches (from £1.40) to steak and kidney pie (£3.95), sweet and sour pork (£4.45) and home-cooked ham (£3.95). The restaurant menu offers interesting fish choices such as the Swan seafood special (£8.95), Dover sole (£11.95), rock eel (£6.95) and steaks and grills (from £8.50).
Times: 12-2.30pm and 7-10.30pm (Sun 12-2pm and 7-9.30pm). Telephone: 0787 222353.

 L eave the pub and retrace your steps to the farm buildings, then keep straight ahead with the farm buildings on your left and climb the stile beyond them. Follow a well marked footpath through fields via stiles, disregarding the path arrowed left. Pass a lake on your right and some woods and a stream to your left and shortly enter pasture. Ignore the defined cattle path and proceed straight across the field to a gate and yellow waymarker. Climb the gate, keep straight ahead to a stile and fingerpost at the end of a wooden fence and join the drive to Swanscombe Farm. Just before the farm, follow the arrowed path to the left of the garden to a stile. Head across fields into a mill yard, turn right at the mill, cross the river and head towards the first pylon. Take the left-hand path under the pylon, then bear right at a fork to follow the path through small fields via stiles, with the river to your left. Eventually pass through a gate and between houses to a road. Turn left, then take the first left opposite the priory, into Ley Road.

Swan Inn
Swan Lane, Chappel,
Colchester, just off A604.

FURTHER EXPLORATION

East Anglian Railway Museum, Chappel
A fascinating collection of period railway architecture and engineering spanning 100 years of railway history, the museum also has various steam days throughout the year. Open daily. Telephone: 0206 242524.

Colchester Zoo, Colchester
Set in over 40 acres of gardens it houses over 150 species of animals, falconry displays, amusement complex, adventure play areas and various special events. Telephone: 0839 222000

Colchester Castle Museum, Colchester
The museum is housed in the largest Norman keep in Europe, which is built over remains of a Roman temple destroyed by Queen Boadicea in AD60.
Telephone 0206 712913

GREAT BARDFIELD
~to~ FINCHINGFIELD

APPROXIMATELY 4 MILES

A gentle walk through very picturesque countryside and incorporating two charming and unspoilt villages.

Parking
OS Map 167 Ref TL6730.
Parking available close to the monument in the centre of Great Bardfield

Fox
Finchingfield - on B1053 between Braintree and Saffron Walden.

Take the footpath along the right-hand side of The Vine pub to a stile at the rear of the pub garden, then head diagonally left downhill passing through a gap in the hedge to an iron gate. Climb the gate, bear half-right downhill to a stile in the field corner, then disregard the stiles to your left and continue ahead over two stiles, a small bridge and across a pasture to a stile in the far left-hand corner. Turn right onto a defined path along the field edge and soon cross the river on your right. Keep the river to your left and cross pastures to a waymarked footpath just beyond a brick-built electricity sub-station. Turn right along the path, left at a road then shortly right into a lane marked Pitley Farm. Turn right at the second footpath sign, bear diagonally right across a field (follow field edge if in crop) to cross a farm track in the far corner. Follow the waymarkers left, cross a ditch, pass through a hedge, then keep left along the field edge and shortly pass through the hedge again. Turn left, then right onto a farm track and keep right at a fork for the track into Finchingfield. The pub lies opposite the green.

⇔*Fox (Free House)*⇔

Located in the heart of this pretty village, opposite the pond and green, this friendly, welcoming 18th-century pub is popular with visitors. It has an attractive pargetted façade and a comfortable interior characterised by beams, brick, copper and old wooden tables. Children are welcome.

On draught: Greene King IPA, Abbot Ale and Rayments Bitter, Harp, Carling Black Label, Kronenbourg, Dry Blackthorn cider.
Food: the simple menu includes soup (£1.25), lasagne (£4.75), quiche and jacket potato (£4.75), steak and kidney pie (£4.25), ploughman's (from £3.50) and filled jacket potatoes (from £2.95).
Times: 11.30am-2.15pm and 7-9.30pm. Open 11am-11pm in summer. Telephone: 0371 810151.

———◆•✦•◆———

From the pub walk along the left-hand side of Bardfield Road, shortly to turn left along footpath No 41, located beside a 30mph sign. Almost immediately turn right (do not cross the bridge), then with the river to your left follow a path through woods and across meadows via stiles. Pass through a gate, cross a track and further fields, heading towards a white windmill. Keep the river on your left, then on nearing the windmill at a fork, ignore the stile on your left and take the right-hand path along the edge of a field to an iron bridge. Cross this and the brick bridge beyond, then follow the path through a gate and between buildings. Immediately behind the cottage turn right (not waymarked) onto a path through a small orchard, with conifers on your left. Go through a gate, cross a stile and follow the path towards Great Bardfield. Pass behind some houses, then at the point where the path begins to climb (windmill to left), turn right at a fork of paths into the village, turning right back to the monument and your car.

FURTHER EXPLORATION

Finchingfield
Possibly the most picturesque village in Essex with a church on a hill, a stream with a duckpond, hump-backed bridge, post mill and green, with buildings of all shapes, sizes and periods, the most notable being the long, white, timber-framed guildhall.

Hedingham Castle, Castle Hedingham
A majestic Norman castle built in 1140, with one of the finest and best preserved keeps in England, standing 100ft high. There are also woodland walks and a lake. Telephone: 0787 60261.

Colne Valley Railway and Museum, Castle Hedingham
Railway buildings contain seven steam locomotives and forty other engines, carriages and wagons. There are steam days, and a five-acre riverside nature and picnic area. Telephone: 0787 61174.

Audley End House, Audley End
A grand 17th-century house built by Thomas Howard, Earl of Suffolk. Fine pictures and furnishings in state rooms. Miniature railway. Telephone: 0799 522399.

HASLINGFIELD ~to~ BARRINGTON

**APPROXIMATELY
6 MILES**

*This is a pleasant
undulating walk
across farmland and
through riverside
meadows.*

Start of walk
OS Map 154 Ref TL4153.
Church Street.

Royal Oak
Barrington, Cambridge - off
A10 Cambridge to Royston
road.

FURTHER EXPLORATION

**Wimpole Hall,
Wimpole**
A grand mansion set in 360
acres of parkland, Wimpole
dates back to 1640. Its Home
Farm displays farm machinery
and implements over the past
200 years, rare breeds of
domestic animals and has a
children's corner and woodland
play area. (National Trust)
Telephone: 0223 207257.

With the church to your left follow Church Street, keeping straight ahead where it curves left on a metalled road which peters out into a track. On reaching Harston Road turn left. Shortly, turn right along a footpath waymarked Hauxton and soon follow a stream and cross a bridge. At a fork, keep right, then the path becomes a lane, and just beyond an old cemetery and phone box (half a mile) turn right into Haslingfield Road. Cross the river, turning left onto a pleasant track beside a line of chestnut trees, then on entering a field, turn left and walk along the river bank. Follow the waymarkers, passing the cement works, after which your track soon becomes metalled as it enters Barrington. At the T-junction, turn right towards the church, pass a duck pond, then turn left over the village green for the pub.

⊸*Royal Oak (Free House)*⊸

This popular, old-world, thatched and beamed pub, dating back to the 14th century, consists of several rambling and comfortable low-ceilinged rooms filled with brasses, harnesses, bric-à-brac and traditional furniture. A huge brick fireplace is a feature of the bar, there is a neat conservatory and plenty of outdoor seating. Children are welcome in the top bar.

On draught: Adnams Bitter, Greene King IPA and Abbot Ale, Flowers Original, Guinness, Fosters, Stella Artois, Dry Blackthorn cider.
Food: the menu includes sandwiches (from £1.85), rack of lamb with rosemary and redcurrant sauce, lasagne, Italian smoked fish with tagliatelle (£5.35-£7.90), vegetarian dishes such as vegetable and basil strudel (£5.95) and cashew Capri with herb and tomato sauce (£5.35).
Times: 12-2pm and 6.30-10pm. Telephone: 0223

From the pub turn right, then at the village sign, head left over the green towards the cricket pavilion. Take the waymarked bridleway across a stile and shortly turn left onto a footpath, signed Harlton/Haslingfield. Keep to the field edge (yellow markers), continue straight past Wilsmere Down Farm on your right and cross a gravel track. Continue along a track that curves round the field, then on reaching some trees, turn right onto a footpath and follow the waymarkers round the edge of a field to the top edge of an enormous limestone quarry. (A parallel path winds through the trees to the left of the quarry-edge path, but it may be overgrown in summer.) Eventually you will reach a stile and a road where you turn left and keep on downhill for the return to Haslingfield, the church and the start of the walk.

Duxford Air Museum, Duxford

The former Battle of Britain fighter station now houses the Imperial War Museum's collection of military aircraft, armoured vehicles and other large exhibits. Over 120 aircraft, and an exciting programme of flying displays and special events. Open all year. Telephone: 0223 835000.

$\mathcal{C}$ASTLETON CIRCULAR $\mathcal{W}$ALK

APPROXIMATELY 4½ MILES

A fascinating walk through a typical limestone landscape, affording magnificent views and the opportunity to visit the hidden underground 'show caves'. Walking boots essential.

Parking

OS Map 110 Ref SK1483. Main car park (charge) or in square near the church in Castleton.

Ye Old Nags Head

Castleton, near Chapel-en-le-Frith - village centre.

FURTHER EXPLORATION
Castleton

A thriving tourist village nestling below the ruins of Peveril Castle, a dominant Norman castle where Henry II accepted the submission of Malcolm king of Scotland in 1157 (open all year). Below the castle is the awesome mouth of Peak Cavern, one of the most spectacular natural limestone caves in the Peak District. (Open daily Etr to Oct). St Edmund's church, though heavily restored in 1837,

$\mathcal{G}$o along Castle Street, bear left across Market Square into Bargate and take the footpath right, waymarked Cave Dale. Cross stile and proceed steadily uphill along the dry valley bottom path with the ruins of Peveril Castle to your right. Ignore paths left and right as you continue through a couple of gates and gradually reach the large pasture on top of the plateau. Pass a small pond, cross a stile beside a gate and turn immediately right over a wall stile on to an established track. In a short distance bear right at fork on to a further waymarked track. Cross a stile and proceed past Rowters Farm to follow metalled driveway down to a gate and B-road. Good views across to Mam Tor. Turn right along verge and keep right on to the lane signed Castleton Caverns. Just beyond farm and cattle grid at the top of the magnificent Winnats Pass (NT), cross stile on left and follow waymarked path left around rear of farm. At a fingerpost turn right, signed Blue John Cavern and shortly descend on grassy path to a stile, gift shop and entrance to the famous cave. Cross ladder stile beside gate and soon drop down to stile (yellow arrows). Join a narrow path that gradually descends hillside (care to be taken), with splendid views along Hope Dale, to a further stile. Drop down steps, pass entrance to Treak Cliff Cavern and follow concrete path for a short way before bearing off right on to defined path across hillside to a stile. Descend steeply left, pass through car park to Speedwell Cavern and cross lane to a stile into High Peak Estate (NT). Follow path through metal gate and keep left alongside dry-stone wall back into Castleton.

$\backsim$ *Ye Olde Nag's Head* (*Free House*)$\backsim$

A civilised 17th-century coaching inn located in the heart of this popular Peak village. The single comfortable bar boasts exposed beams, a collection of antique tables and chairs, fresh flowers, quality prints, paintings and fabrics and a warming winter fire. Attractive adjacent restaurant and eight ensuite bedrooms. No children under 14 and no muddy boots or packs in the bar.

On draught: Boddingtons Bitter, Bass, Guinness, Carling Black Label, Skol, Tennants Extra, Dry Blackthorn cider.

Food: a wide-ranging bar menu lists sandwiches (from £1.95), smoked salmon on rye (£4.10), steak and kidney pie, lasagne (both £4.95), dressed crab Creole (£5.50), cod fillet (£5.45), roast beef and Yorkshire pudding (£5.50), leek and mushroom crumble and nut Wellington (both £5.35). More elaborate and expensive meals in the restaurant.

Times: 12-2.45pm and 7-10.30pm, restaurant 12-2pm (2.30pm Sun) and 7-10pm. Pub open 11am-11pm, except Sun. Telephone: 0433 621604.

retains 17th-century box pews, a fine Norman chancel arch and a valuable library.

Blue John Cavern and Mine

A fine example of a water-worn cave with chambers 200ft high. It contains 8 of the 14 veins of Blue John stone and has been a major source of this unique form of fluorspar for nearly 300 years. Open daily all year. Telephone: 0433 620638.

Speedwell Cavern

Visitors descend 105 steps to a boat which takes them on a one-mile exploration of the floodlit cavern. Open daily all year. Telephone: 0433 620512.

$\mathcal{C}$HATSWORTH ~to~ $\mathcal{R}$OWSLEY

From the car park follow the lane right, passing Chatsworth Garden Centre and Sawmill into the estate hamlet of Calton Lees. At a fork bear off right onto a gravel track (blue arrow) and remain on this peaceful route gradually uphill parallel to a small brook. Pass between dwellings (Calton Houses) to a gate and turn left with blue arrow alongside coniferous woodland. Shortly, pass between woods to a gate and bear left on defined track marked with blue arrows, uphill across pasture to a ladder stile and enter woodland. Follow path through a clearing and further trees, go through old gateway and proceed on path steadily downhill through coniferous and later beech woods to a T-junction of paths. Turn left, then in a little way bear right, signed Bakewell and descend to a crossroads of tracks. Turn left through a metal barrier onto a track, waymarked Rowsley. Keep right at a fork of paths, proceed along woodland edge and continue downhill into Rowsley, The track soon becomes metalled and passes the church to the A6. Turn left along footway to the pub.

Leave the pub, retrace steps back up the lane beside the Peacock Hotel and take the waymarked path right to Chatsworth, just beyond Granby Cottage. Pass beneath the old railway and follow the track parallel to River Derwent to a gate. Remain on the track (can be muddy), pass through an old gateway and keep left on a worn grassy path to a stile. Continue through scrub, climb a stile, bear left with yellow arrow across pasture and rejoin river edge, then bear half-left across the field to a gate. Bear left uphill to a ladder stile, turn right along the wall to a further stile and proceed ahead along the lane through Calton Lees back to car park.

❧ *Grouse and Claret* (Mansfield) ❧

Attractively refurbished 18th-century roadside pub with traditional Tap Room and a comfortable, well decorated and furnished lounge bar and adjacent conservatory. Collection of framed fishing flies and old and new prints adorn the walls. Separate family bar and an imaginative and safe children's play area. Overnight accommodation in five bedrooms.

On draught: Mansfield Best Bitter, Riding Bitter and Old Baily, Riding Mild, Guinness, Fosters, McEwan, Woodpecker cider. **Food:** a carvery serves hot-plate specials (all £4.25) - Old Baily beef, game pie, meat and potato, steak and kidney pudding - steaks (£7.95), mixed grill (£8.95), seafood platter (£5.75) and choice of vegetarian meals (£4.25). Snacks include soup (£1.95), large filled rolls (£2.50) and ploughman's (£3.95). Traditional Sunday roast (£4.25).

Times: Bar open 11am-11pm, breakfast available from 8.30am. Bar meals: 12-2.30pm and 6-9.30pm, all day Sat and Sun. Telephone: 0629 733233.

Chatsworth

The palatial home of the Duke and Duchess of Devonshire boasts one of the richest collections of fine decorative arts in private hands. The stately rooms are magnificently decorated and furnished. The vast parkland was laid out by 'Capability' Brown and later Sir Joseph Paxton, who added the Cascade and the Emperor Fountain. Adventure playground. Open late Mar to Oct. Telephone: 0246 582204.

Stanton Moor
(1¼ miles south)

An isolated island of gritstone rising to 1,096ft with more than 70 barrows and cairns and an interesting stone circle known as The Nine Ladies.

$\mathcal{C}$ALVER ~to~ $\mathcal{F}$ROGGATT EDGE

APPROXIMATELY 4 MILES

An enjoyable varied and scenic walk along the high and exposed Curbar Edge offering splendid views, returning to Calver along the peaceful riverside path beside the River Derwent.

From your car head towards the Bridge Inn and turn right up Curbar Lane, beside the church. Proceed steeply uphill through the village, following Bar Road and take fourth waymarked path right, where lane curves left and go through a squeeze stile. Shortly, enter Curbar Gap (NT) and continue uphill to cross a stile to rejoin the lane. Turn right for a short distance before bearing left on to a stony track, and curve right uphill to wooden gate. Join a well worn track across the top of Curbar Edge with outstanding views. Remain on track for nearly a mile to a small wooden post, where you bear off left on to a path beneath rocky crags. Look out for an ill defined path on your left that descends steeply through woodland to a stile. Continue downhill to a road and right for the pub.

❧*Chequers Inn* (Wards)❧

Originally four cottages, this traditional inn offers a warm welcome within its tastefully decorated main bar, which features waxed floorboards, stone fireplace with woodburner, an assortment of chairs and settles and attractive antique prints. Popular at all times; booking advisable for restaurant. Six individually furnished bedrooms and splendid views from the terraced woodland garden. Children welcome in restaurant.

On draught: Wards Best Bitter, Vaux Samson Bitter, Thorne Best Bitter, Guinness, Carlsberg, Labatts, good range of wines by the glass and a collection of malt whiskies. **Food:** a hearty range of value-for-money bar meals include sandwiches (from £1.95), steak and mushroom pie (£4.65), rabbit and fennel pie (£4.25), oxtail and vegetable casserole (£4.95) and daily specials such as game and oyster pie (£4.65), grilled fillet of Scotch salmon (£5.10) and home-made cauliflower soup (£1). Puddings include traditional Bakewell pudding (£3.85). Set dinner in restaurant (£14.45). **Times:** 12-2pm and 6-9.30pm (Sun 12-2.30pm and 7-9.30pm).
Telephone: 0433 630231

❖━◆━❖

*L*eave the pub, cross the road and turn left downhill to a wall stile near a gate. Descend on arrowed grassy path between trees to a squeeze stile on to a lane. Turn right, then as the road curves right climb a wall stile to your left on to the riverside path beside the River Derwent. Remain on this peaceful defined path, and shortly cross B-road beside bridge and maintain course alongside river to a narrow lane. Turn right to the Bridge Inn and your car.

Parking
OS Map 119 Ref SK2474. Large layby beside A623 towards Baslow, near Calver Mill and beside primary school.

Chequers Inn
Froggatt Edge, near Calver - on B6054 north of Calver.

FURTHER EXPLORATION

Calver
The village stands on the River Derwent, which is spanned by an 18th-century bridge. It is overlooked by an austere Georgian cotton mill which was used as Colditz Castle in the TV series 'Colditz'. North of the village are Curbar Edge and Froggatt Edge, areas of woodland, meadow and pasture affording magnificent views across the Derwent Valley.

Chatsworth
Chatsworth is the palatial home of the Duke and Duchess of Devonshire and has one of the richest collections of fine and decorative arts in private hands. Splendid painted hall, wall and ceiling paintings, magnificent pictures, porcelain and furniture. Fine parkland laid out by 'Capability' Brown and Sir Joseph Paxton, who added the Cascade and the Emperor Fountain, which sends up a jet of water to 290ft. Adventure playground and numerous events. Open daily late Mar to Oct. Telephone: 0246 582204.

ᗡIMMINGSDALE ~to~ ᗅLTON

XIMATELY
4 MILES**

An undulating walk exploring the Churnet Valley and the delightful wooded Dimmingsdale with splendid views across rolling Staffordshire countryside.

Parking
OS Map 119 Ref SK0643. Forestry Commission parking area on narrow lane between Alton and Oakamoor.

Bulls Head Inn
High Street, Alton, near Cheadle. Village centre.

FURTHER EXPLORATION

Dimmingsdale
One of Staffordshire's most enchanting valleys, covered with ancient woodland and offering a wealth of wildlife and scenic paths. Once famous for its lead and iron ore industry the area was eventually transformed by the Earl of Shrewsbury, who removed the spoil heaps and landscaped the valley with magnificent drives, now incorporated into a walk.

From the car park follow a gravel track past Ramblers Retreat, keeping left of the mill and lake on a woodland path. Take the third arrowed path left at a lake, waymarked Gentleman's Rock. Shortly, at a post, follow red arrow for Threape Wood and climb steeply uphill through woodland. At a post with a yellow arrow, turn left along a path to a squeeze stile on woodland fringe. Proceed across two fields via squeeze stiles to a B-road. Turn right, cross onto a tree-lined track, then just before buildings, cross a stile on the left and head diagonally left with a line of telegraph poles to a stile beside a gate. Bear half-left to a fence stile, keep ahead on the track to a gate, then head slightly left across pasture to a stile hidden in the hedgerow. Keep left to a squeeze stile in the field corner and maintain direction along edge of fields via fence stiles and gates, parallel to a track, to a B-road opposite Broad View. Cross over, turn right along the verge, then left downhill at a crossroads of lanes at Gallows Green. Enter Alton, keeping ahead at the junction near a stone lock-up and turn right into the High Street for the pub.

ᥫᎮ*Bulls Head Inn* (Free House)ᥫᎮ

A homely 18th-century inn in the village centre with a cosy main bar with beamed ceiling, brick fireplace with open fire, church pew seating and comfortable easy chairs and stools. Children are welcome away from the bar and in the separate restaurant. Overnight accommodation is available.
On draught: Tetley Bitter, Bass, Guinness, Skol, Lowenbrau, Carling Black Label, Gaymers Old Original cider. **Food:** standard selection of bar meals include pâté (£2.25), soup (£1.75), sandwiches - ham (£1.95), omelettes (£3.75), savoury pancake rolls (£4.25), mushroom and nut fettucine (£4.95), lasagne (£5.25), fillet steak (£9.95) and mushroom stroganoff (£4.25).

Times: 12-2pm (except Sat and Sun) and 7-9pm (9.30pm Fri and Sat). No food all day Tue. Telephone: 0538 702065.

*R*eturn to the lock-up, turn right downhill and proceed over a T-junction onto a waymarked path beside the Royal Oak. Keep to the track then at a junction of arrowed paths, turn right, then left beside the gate with Staffordshire Way signs and bear right down to a stile on woodland fringe. Continue downhill to a lane, keep ahead and take the track left, signed Dimmingsdale and Smelting Mill. Enter woodland, look out for a path/gully on your right (not waymarked) and descend to the car park.

The old mill, built around 1741, survives, as do the ponds which drove the water-wheels.

Alton Towers
This popular theme park set in 200 acres of landscaped gardens, offers a unique blend of wild roller coasters, thrilling family rides and stunning live shows to make a day of excitement and fun. Attractions open daily mid Mar to early Nov, grounds and gardens open daily all year. Telephone: 0538 702200.

TEGG'S NOSE COUNTRY PARK
~to~ LANGLEY

APPROXIMATELY 4 MILES

A short, quite strenuous ramble through undulating farmland and forest with a long steep climb up Tegg's Nose that is rewarded by unrivalled open views.

Parking
OS Map 118 Ref SJ9573. Large car park and picnic area at Tegg's Nose Country Park, east of Macclesfield.

Leather's Smithy
Langley, near Macclesfield - in village fork left at church into Clarke lane for ½ mile to pub.

FURTHER EXPLORATION

Gawsworth Hall, Gawsworth
This fine Tudor black-and-white manor was the birthplace of Mary Fitton, thought by some to be the 'Dark Lady' of Shakespeare's sonnets. Pictures and armour can be seen in the house, which also has a tilting ground - now thought to be a rare example of an Elizabethan

From the car park take stony path by County Council sign, signed Langley. Head steeply downhill with splendid views, pass through a gate, then on merging with a lane keep straight on, shortly to bear left, waymarked Forest Chapel. Ascend on pathway beside stone house, bear right and remain on this rough path which undulates across the hillside. At a fork, keep left with main path to a farmhouse and driveway. Turn right, then shortly bear off right to a stile and enter Macclesfield Forest. Follow delightful path, bearing right at fingerpost to pass a stone barn to a crossroads of waymarked tracks. Turn right on to a wide track, signed Langley, following it downhill through woodland. On nearing a wooden gate, bear left through a swing gate, turn right on to a lane and follow it to the pub.

⇔Leather's Smithy (Tetley)⇔

Isolated among sheep pastures, forests and hills this friendly stone-built 18th-century pub overlooks Ridgegate Reservoir and is a popular destination for both anglers and walkers. Bare flagged stone floor, a warming open fire, low beams and comfortable seating feature in the walkers' bar. Other visitors can also settle in the adjacent cosy, carpeted bar. Family room and garden.

On draught: Jennings Bitter and Sneck Lifter, Tetley Bitter, Ind Coope Burton Ale, Guinness, Skol, Lowenbrau, Castlemaine XXXX, Addlestones cider, over 65 malt whiskies and gluwein in winter. **Food:** a good value menu features country vegetable soup (£1.50), sandwiches (from £1.65), beef pie (£3.20), chilli (£4.40), roast beef (£6) and a selection of vegetarian dishes - wheat and walnut casserole (£4.25). Puddings (£2) include raspberry and redcurrant pie and trifle. **Times:** 12-2pm and 7-8.30pm (9.30pm Fri and Sat). No food Mon evening. Telephone: 0260 252313

From the pub follow the lane right, then on nearing end of small reservoir by some cottages, bear off right on to footpath, waymarked Tegg's Nose. Cross the head of reservoir and footbridge, climb some steps to a gate and track. Bear left, then right with Gritstone Trail sign beside further reservoir before turning left through kissing gate into Tegg's Nose Country Park. Follow yellow waymarker and climb up a long steep worn path (frequent benches) to a stile and track. Turn right for viewpoint. Follow track left, pass through wooden gate on your right and follow stony track uphill to another gate. Beyond, turn left through disused quarry following path past old machinery display and keep right down some stony steps to pass through a gate on your right. Follow track back to the car park.

pleasure garden. Open Apr to early Oct. Telephone: 0260 223456.

Macclesfield
An old silk-manufacturing town full of character, from its steep streets to its 18th and 19th-century mills. The silk museum presents the story of silk in the town through various exhibitions and models and is situated in the Heritage Centre (open all year, telephone 0625 613210). A further museum relating to silk production can be found in Paradise Mill, a working mill until 1981 when the last handloom weaver retired. 26 handlooms have been restored and exhibitions give impressions of working conditions in 1930's. (open all year, telephone 0625 618228).

ELTON ~to~ FOTHERINGHAY

**APPROXIMATELY
5 MILES**

*An easy going walk
with open views over
parkland and
meadows.*

Parking

OS Map 142 Ref TL1893. On
the east side of B671 south of
Elton church or in the village.

*G*o through the churchyard to a kissing-gate in
the far left corner and bear right through the
grass parkland. Turn right beyond the first wooden
gate and head diagonally right downhill to a stile and
surfaced track. Turn left, pass through a metal gate and
follow the bridleway skirting Elton Park. On reaching a
further stile and bridge, proceed straight on into
woodland (can be overgrown). In a few yards take a
path left onto adjoining field and follow the woodland
edge. Shortly, walk towards the distinctive spire of
Warmington church and reach the A605. Turn right,
pass the Red Lion and take the footpath right,
waymarked Fotheringhay. Bear half-right across
pasture, pass behind houses and through an old
orchard to reach a derelict water mill and the River
Nene. Cross a stile, bear right for a prominent wooden
bridge and proceed towards the lock on the well

waymarked Nene Way. Continue on defined path across lush meadowland towards Fotheringhay, passing the remains of the Castle as you enter the village. Turn right for the pub, situated on the left beyond the church.

⊸*Falcon Inn (Free House)*⊸

This popular, stone built, 18th-century pub stands opposite the imposing village church. A comfortable and friendly atmosphere pervades in the well frequented public bar and the comfortably furnished lounge and airy conservatory, which bustle with visitors seeking out the notable food. The colourful, well tended garden and patio are ideal for summer drinking. Children are very welcome.

On draught: Adnams Bitter, Elgoods Cambridge Bitter, Greene King IPA and Abbot, Ruddles County, and also a good selection of wines. **Food:** an imaginative range of home-cooked dishes may include French onion soup (£2.30), fresh Grimsby cod and prawns au gratin (£6.80), African boboti (£4.80), roast duckling with orange and almonds (£6) and braised rabbit Provençale (£6). Sandwiches (from £2) and puddings (from £2.30). Cold buffet weekend lunchtimes.

Times: 12.15-2pm and 6.30-9.30pm (7-9pm Sun). No bar food Mon. Summer afternoon teas 3-5pm Telephone: 08326 254.

------◆◆◆◆------

From the inn take the Nassington road opposite the church and after crossing a small brook take the waymarked path on the right. Proceed on the well marked path through two fields to Middle Lodge, an unoccupied brick farmyard. Continue along the gravel track behind the buildings to a crossroads and turn right towards the outline of Elton church. Cultivated farmland gives way to grassy meadows, cross the weir by a metal bridge and the lock to enter Elton by the green. Turn right, then right again into Chapel Lane and rejoin the footpath leading back to the churchyard.

Falcon Inn
Fotheringhay, near Peterborough. Village signposted off A605, 4 miles north-east of Oundle.

FURTHER EXPLORATION

Fotheringhay
An attractive village where once stood the historic Fotheringhay Castle in which Richard of York (later King Richard III) was born and where Mary, Queen of Scots was beheaded in 1587. Only the motte and bailey remains. A magnificent 15th-century church dominates the village but what one sees today is only a portion of a much larger foundation.

Elton Hall,
Elton
Parts of the present Jacobean house built by Sir Thomas Proby date back to 1660 and there is a fine collection of pictures and a library. Open Sun, Bank Hols and some weekdays in summer.

Prebendal Manor House,
Nassington
This is the earliest surviving manor house in the county dating from the early 13th century. Open: Tue, Wed and Sun June to Aug and Bank Hols.

WARTNABY ~to~ OLD DALBY

**APPROXIMATELY
5¼ MILES**

A pleasant, bright and breezy walk with some short ups and downs.

Start of walk
OS Map 129 Ref SK7122. Limited parking near Wartnaby church.

Crown
Debdale Hill, Old Dalby, near Melton Mowbray - village off A606 and A6006 north-west of Melton Mowbray.

FURTHER EXPLORATION

Wartnaby
Wartnaby In old English Wartnaby meant 'watch-hill', a look-out post which commands fine views northwards over the Trent Valley. Charles II is supposed to have breakfasted at Wartnaby Hall.

Walk downhill from the church, pass the entrance to Wartnaby Hall and locate the telephone box. Follow a broad bridleway past a farmyard, and arable fields to a road. Cross over via the stile and gate to the right, proceed across pasture (hawthorn hedge to right) and follow the track past a farmyard to a gate on the right. Continue into the village of Grimston, passing the pub into Perkins Lane. After 300 yards take the waymarked path right through the centre of a field, parallel with the lane. (If the field is in crop it maybe more practical to stay on the lane). At the end of the field cross the B676, enter Old Dalby Wood and follow a well worn path through the wood and up a grassy slope before passing below Dalby Hall. Go through a gate, turn left along a tarmac lane, cross the main road and follow the footpath straight on to approach the back of the Crown.

Crown *(Free House)*

Tucked away down a lane in the village centre, this 300-year-old converted farmhouse remains unspoilt with a series of cosy tiny rooms, each with its own open fire, low beams, various antique furnishings and quality fabrics and paintings. The gardens have a delightful rear lawn and terrace, plus a croquet and petanque pitch. Children are welcome except in the front bar.

On draught: a constantly changing selection of up to 10 ales Marstons Best Bitter, Batemans XB, Adnams Broadside, Morland Old Speckled Hen, Kimberley Classic - Carlsberg and Export, Strongbow cider, good wines and whiskies. **Food:** Imaginative, freshly prepared and well presented dishes may include avocado, prawns and raspberry viniagrette (£4.95), Welsh rarebit (£3.95), lamb steak with herb sauce (£9.95) and medallions of fillet beef with real ale sauce

(£13.95). Sandwiches and rolls (from £2.75). Puddings (£3) include Sicilian trifle and chocolate fudge cake. Sunday lunch is served and there is a separate restaurant.

Times: 12-2pm and 6.30-10pm, except Sun evening and restricted menu Mon evening. Telephone: 0664 823134.

From the pub retrace your steps past the church and the earlier footpath and locate a further waymarked footpath on the right. Initially narrow and slightly overgrown, soon cross pasture to a gate in the far left-hand corner. Proceed uphill on a track to a wooden fenced area (army depot left, aerial right), then head east downhill across pasture to a stile. Continue straight on (private woods right), then at the top of the rise bear left and follow power wires to a road. Cross over, go through the gate to the left and head towards a prominent grass ridge. With farm buildings in sight, keep them well to the left as you bear diagonally right through a field to the main road. Turn left towards houses, shortly cross over to take waymarked footpath towards Wartnaby. Aim for the pylon and rooves of houses, or skirt around the field if in crop, to reach Wartnaby and your car.

Melton Mowbray

An old market town and unofficial capital of the hunting country, where three hunts meet - the Quorn, the Cottesmore and the Belvoir. Classics of English food - the renowned pork pies, Hunt Cake, Stilton cheese and Red Leicester can be seen being made locally. The town is attractively located on the River Eye and St Mary's Church is arguably the stateliest and most impressive of all the county's churches, and beautifully illustrates the early-English, decorated and perpendicular architectural periods.

C RANOE ~to~ H ALLATON

**APPROXIMATELY
4¼ MILES**

*An easy-to-follow
walk with marvellous
panoramic views over
the most pleasant hill
countryside of East
Leicestershire. Well
waymarked by yellow
posts.*

In the lane behind Cranoe church take the
waymarked bridleway to Goadby Road. Climb a
grassy hill to the top left corner of the field, passing
yellow posts to an iron gate. Keep to the hedge with
unspoilt open views. Pass a small pond on the right to
a gate and a view over fine hunting country. Proceed
slightly right across pasture to a post and gate, then
keep to the right-hand side of the hedge to reach a
broad firm track (Goadby Road). Turn right, head due
east passing fields and a line of willows to the right in
a stream. Cross the stream with old motte and bailey to
right, then where the track bears left, take the arrowed
path right across pasture towards Hallaton church.
Pass the cemetry and church to the green with its
ancient buttercross and pub opposite.

⊶*Bewicke Arms* (Free House)⊷

This pretty 400-year-old thatched inn stands by the green in this attractive unspoilt village. Two welcoming beamed bars with warming open fires are comfortably furnished with old-fashioned settles and oak tables and various farming implements adorn the walls. Charming flower-decked terrace and lawn with play area and pen for chickens and hens. Children welcome inside. Overnight accommodation.

On draught: Ruddles Best Bitter and County, Marston's Pedigree, Webster's Yorkshire Bitter, Guinness, Fosters, Strongbow and Woodpecker cider. **Food:** reliable home-cooked food may include baked mussels in garlic (£3.90), soup (£1.95), beery beef casserole (£6.40), cheesy chicken (£7.90) and Burgundy beef cooked in red wine and onions (£6.80). Snacks listed are salads (£5.20), ploughman's (£3.60) and sandwiches (from £1.40). Banana and toffee pie and fruit flan (£2.40) for dessert.
Times: 12-2pm and 7.30-9.45pm. Telephone: 085889 217.

———◆◆◆———

From the pub retrace your steps to the church, pass the cemetery and locate the familiar yellow post with circular sign. Climb the stile, turn left (below the motte and bailey can be seen the outline presumably, of the old ironworks the castle was built to protect), then on reaching a double stile, bear right with yellow arrow across a field with a deep pond up to the left, towards another yellow post. Descend a large field, cross the bridge over the stream and head south-west through a field towards Othorpe House. Pass to the right of the house and farmyard, cross a field and gently climb up to a yellow post. Follow the lower of the two waymarkers along the field hedge and down a grassy field behind Cranoe Old Rectory, back to your starting point.

Start of walk
OS 141 Ref SK7896. Cranoe church

Bewicke Arms
1 Eastgate, Hallaton, near Market Harborough.
The village is signposted from B664 south-west of Uppingham.

FURTHER EXPLORATION

Hallaton

This old village set in pleasant hill country has a quaint conical market cross and a well preserved terrace of 17th to 19th-century stone-built cottages. A curious local custom is the Easter Monday's hare-pie scramble. This entails the distribution of a large hare-pie to local residents - originally a token rent for a field. A second ritual, 'bottle-kicking' involves residents from surrounding villages competing to push two small casks of beer - or bottles - over a local stream. The beer is later drunk at the market cross in the village.

GRIMBLETHORPE
~to~ DONINGTON-ON-BAIN

**APPROXIMATELY
5¼ MILES**

*A gently undulating
walk through
picturesque Wolds
countryside,
incorporating part of
the long-distance path
called The Viking
Way.*

Parking
OS Map 122 Ref TF2386. Large
layby beside A157 in the
hamlet of Grimblethorpe
between Lincoln and Louth.

Black Horse
Donington-on-Bain, near Louth.
Village lies between the A153
and A157 south-west of Louth.

FURTHER EXPLORATION

Viking Way
This long-distance path
traverses the Lincolnshire
Wolds from the Humber Bridge
to Oakham in Leicestershire, a
total of 140 miles.

The Wolds
A 40-mile stretch of chalk
uplands that belies the
common belief that
Lincolnshire is simply an
extension of the Fens.

*C*ross the main road onto a lane waymarked to Gayton le Wold and shortly take an arrowed path left over a double stile into pasture. Keep right-handed to a stile, cross a farm track and proceed ahead to two stiles and a footbridge over a stream. Bear diagonally left across pasture to a stile in the field corner, then follow a defined path across the field towards a silo to reach a farm track. Cross over, pass through a gate and bear left through centre of pasture behind Grange Farm to a stile beside a gate. Turn right around the field edge, cross arrowed stile on right and head uphill across an open field towards a tall mast and a farm track. Turn left and follow a waymarked route to a lane. Turn right along the verge, pass entrance to Glebe Farm, gently descend and take signed path left alongside the farmyard. Climb a stile on the right, cross a track and another stile, then turn left along field edge and shortly cross a plank bridge into a field. Turn right onto a track beside a hedge, then at arrowed post, turn right along a grassy track between fields and follow arrowed hedged route to the church and village lane. Turn left for the pub.

Black Horse *(Free House)*

This popular walkers' retreat on the Viking Way, nestling in a peaceful Wolds village, has a number of rambling comfortably furnished rooms radiating out from a central low-beamed bar with good open fire. There are a games room, a family room. a patio, a garden and eight attractive ensuite bedrooms. Dogs are not allowed.

On draught: Webster's Yorkshire Bitter, Courage Directors, John Smith's Bitter, Ruddles Best Bitter, Guinness, Fosters, Muller Pilsner, Dry Blackthorn cider. **Food:** generous home-cooked bar meals include steak and kidney pie (£4.75), macaroni cheese (£4.50),

Viking grill (£10.25), filled jacket potatoes (from £1.95), vegetable curry (£4.75), lasagne (£5.25) and traditional Sunday lunch (£4.75). Puddings (£1.95) include apple pie.

Times: 12-2pm and 7-10pm (Sun 9.30pm). Telephone: 0507 343640.

---

*T*urn right on leaving pub, follow the lane out of the village to a fork. Bear right, signed Hallington, then take arrowed footpath left across a stile (Viking Way) onto a defined waymarked track through pastures, parallel to the River Bain. Keep to the path alongside the lake and through a reed area to a stile. Proceed ahead, cross footbridge over river and bear right along the path towards the church to a gate. Bear left around churchyard and cottage to a lane, crossing to a footbridge over a stream. Head diagonally left uphill across pasture to a stile beside woodland and follow the track to a lane. Turn right, pass infill site and turn right with waymarker along the edge of the site to a stile in the left-hand hedge. Bear half-right across pasture to a stile and footbridge in the far corner, then head diagonally left towards a house and a stile. Head right to a stile by a gate and turn left along lane back to main road.

The Wolds contain rolling hills and deep valleys, quiet streams and hanging beechwoods and rise to 552ft. The land is lightly populated, but there is sheep and crop farming.

Louth
A fine market town with a wealth of Georgian and early-Victorian architecture. The church's 295ft perpendicular tower and spire dates from1506 and has a claim to be considered one of the finest in England. Tennyson attended the grammar school, and his first book of poems was published here.

OSBOURNBY ~to~ NEWTON

APPROXIMATELY 5¼ MILES

A gentle walk along good tracks and paths through fertile farmland.

Parking
OS Map 130 Ref TF 0738. Plenty of space in the wide street in Osbournby, just off A15 south of Sleaford.

Red Lion
Newton, near Sleaford - village just off A52 Grantham to Boston road.

FURTHER EXPLORATION

Newton
This stone-built village grew around the rim of a small depression in the limestone heath, at the top of Newton Bar, reputedly the highest point between Grantham and the Urals.

Belton House
Belton (north-east of Grantham)
A handsome mansion in parkland, home to the Brownlow family for 300 years

From the church walk along the main village street and take the waymarked path left just beyond the post office. At an open field, turn left, follow a path around the field edge, enter the field on your left and keep right-handed with yellow arrow to cross a dyke to a gate. Turn right, shortly curve left with a wide track, then at a fingerpost and fork of paths, bear left and keep right through pasture to a waymarked stile. Keep left along the field edge to the main road. Cross over, turn left along the verge and shortly climb a stile in hedge on your right. Turn right around the edge of a large field, gently climbing uphill to a stile and turn right onto a wide grassy track. Follow this into Newton. At the village lane keep straight on to the pub.

☙Red Lion *(Free House)*❧

A charming and friendly village pub with one comfortably furnished bar and adjacent seating areas filled with farm tools, wheels, prints and various bric-à-brac. In summer the terrace is covered with wisteria,and the peaceful garden is pleasant for al fresco eating and drinking. Children are welcome, there is an outdoor play area and, unusually, two squash courts, open to non-members

On draught: Bass, Batemans XXXB, Guinness, Stella Artois, Tennants Pilsner, Strongbow cider.
Food: noted for its exceptional carvery and home-made hot dishes. Fish and cold meat choices with help-yourself salad selection (£6.95-£8.95), soup (£1.90), steak and kidney pie, carbonade of beef, chicken curry, lasagne, turkey, ham and cheese pie (all £5.25), home-made puddings (£2.25). Carvery on Sundays.
Times: 12-2pm and 7-10pm. Telephone: 05297 256.

eave the pub, retrace your steps back past the church and Pump Field House, then turn left across an arrowed stile into a field. Proceed ahead downhill to a junction of paths and cross a stile and footbridge. Continue straight on along edge of two fields to a plank bridge, then bear slightly left across the field with a water tower to your left. Cross another plank bridge over a dyke and proceed along the left-hand hedge downhill to the main road. Cross over onto a lane, waymarked Dembleby, and enter the hamlet, passing the church and Church Farm. Where the lane curves sharp left, bear off right onto wide grassy track and follow it to a metalled lane. Keep straight on for ¾ mile back into Osbournby.

before being given to the National Trust. State rooms feature splendid furnishings, decorations, tapestries, portraits, porcelain and fine furniture. Magnificent rolling grounds and gardens with an orangery and formal 19th-century Italian garden. Open ApR to Oct. Telephone: 0476 66116.

KETTLEWELL ~to~ ARNCLIFFE

APPROXIMATELY
6 MILES

*Strenous in places,
this walk features a
couple of steep ascents
and moorland terrain
between Wharfedale
and Littondale.
Walking boots or
stout walking shoes
are essential*

Parking
OS Map 98 Ref MR9672. Large
public car park at the rear of
the garage in Kettlewell.

Falcon Inn
Arncliffe, Grassington. Off
B6160, 7 miles north-west of
Grassington.

FURTHER EXPLORATION

Kettlewell
One of the most attractive of
Upper Wharfedale's villages,
situated picturesquely among
stone-walled moors with Great
Whernside rising to 2,320ft
nearby.

*L*eave the car park, turn right, cross the River Wharfe, then turn right through the higher of the two gates giving access to the fell side. Soon follow the defined footpath which climbs steadily to the nick in the rocks on the skyline. Continue upwards, crossing a track and a ladder wall stile, then follow the line of the wall, eventually crossing towards an outcrop of rock ahead. The well defined path crosses several ladder wall stiles before bearing right to begin the descent to Arncliffe. Beyond a ladder stile at the face of Park Scar, the path descends the rocky scar through woodland, eventually crossing a road into riverside meadow, giving a view of the ancient parish church. Walk along the riverbank, then cross the river via the road bridge and follow the road to the village green. Turn right to the pub.

Falcon Inn *(Free House)*

Popular with fell walkers, this simple and unspoilt ivy-covered stone-built inn has been in the Miller family for four generations and is charmingly set on the village green. A central hatchway serves two traditional small rooms with settles, cast-iron tables and open fires. Old photographs and watercolours adorn the walls. Children are welcome at lunchtimes in the conservatory. Overnight accommodation and fishing are available.

On draught: Younger's Scotch Bitter.
Food: a small range of generous bar snacks include sandwiches (from £1.35), pie and peas (£1.35) and ploughman's (£2.50).
Times: 12-2pm only, evening dinner for non-residents by prior arrangement. Telephone: 0756 770205.

On leaving the inn cross the village green, retracing your steps to the church. Pass the lych gate and walk between two stone gateposts into a driveway, then go through a gated stile to follow the well worn path along the south bank of the River Skirfare. Shortly, leave the riverbank and continue through meadowland, via stiles, rejoining the river after about a mile, then in a little way cross the river by a metal footbridge.Turn right, following the lane through Hawkeswick, then at a barn, where the road curves right, bear off onto a track that heads up the fell side. Climb steadily, the track becoming a footpath, then at a cairn bear left to follow the pathway over the fell to a ladder stile and begin your descent towards Kettlewell. Enter and skirt the right-hand side of a wood, then turn left after passing a ruined building, the path descending to a gateway giving access to the B6160. Follow the road across the river into Kettlewell and your car.

Arncliffe

Typical grey-stone houses of the Dales area nestle amongst clumps of mature sycamores in this secluded Littondale community. There is a clearly-defined Celtic field system nearby.

Malham Cove

This is one of England's great natural wonders, with its 70-metre- high sheer walls. It was formed by the combined erosional effects of both ice and water on the weak Craven Fault some 12,000 years ago. The result is the beautiful, striking, wide cove with Malham Beck flowing out from the base of the cliff.

ℬURNSALL ~to~ ℒINTON

**APPROXIMATELY
5½ MILES**

*A pleasant country
ramble affording good
views across
Wharfedale, with a
gentle return walk
along the Dales Way,
through meadowland
beside the River
Wharf*

Parking
OS Map 98 Ref MR0361.
Riverside car park (charge) in
Burnsall village.

Fountaine Inn
Linton, Grassington - just off
B6265 Skipton to Grassington
road.

**FURTHER EXPLORATION
Linton**
Charming Dales village with
grey houses grouped around
the village green and Linton
Beck, which is crossed by three
bridges - packhorse, clapper
and a road bridge. Gracefully
dominating the scene is the
imposing façade of Fountaine's
Hospital, an almshouse
founded in 1721 by Richard
Fountaine.

From the car park walk along the main street, turn left at the Red Lion then take the footpath beside a cottage, waymarked to Thorpe. Beyond two gates follow the defined path across meadowland via numerous wall stiles, then cross a farm track and further stiles and fields to Badger Lane. Cross the lane, bear half-left to a ladder stile and cross Starton Beck, then with the wall to your left climb uphill through a gate, over a wall stile onto a green lane. Keep on as far as a metalled lane, turn left into Thorpe, and bear right through the hamlet passing the fine 18th-century manor house. Just beyond Thorpe bear left along a lane, disregard the walled bridleway to the B6160, instead, after about 100 yds, cross a wall stile on the right (sign obscured) and head downhill across a field to a ladder stile in the corner. Make for the gap in the dry-stone wall to join a track leading down through a farmyard, then turn right towards Linton and the pub which overlooks the village green.

❧*Fountaine Inn* (Free House)☙

This welcoming 18th-century pub overlooks the green, a narrow stream and a 14th-century clapper bridge in this delightful little hamlet. Cosy and low ceilinged, the bar is traditionally furnished with old benches, settles, tables and a warmed by an open fire. Children are welcome away from the bar.

On draught: Black Sheep Bitter and Special, Jennings Bitter, Carlsberg.
Food: simple, generously served meals include Linton grill (£10), goulash (£5.25), giant Yorkshire pudding filled with beef and tomato casserole (£5.50), deep-fried seafood platter (£5.25), salads (from £4.75), sandwiches (from £2). Puddings (£2)
Times: 12-2.30pm, 7-9.15pm. Telephone: 0756 752210

$\mathcal{L}$eave the inn, turn left, then right and cross the road bridge. Beyond the village sign, turn right onto a narrow road, then on reaching B6160, bear right for a short distance before taking the footpath on the left towards the River Wharfe. At the roadway near the river bank turn right, shortly to follow the path through the churchyard. Keep to the right-hand wall, entering a riverside meadow and cross the River Wharfe via stepping stones. (To avoid stepping stones, return through churchyard along river bank to cross new footbridge - Tin Bridge - across the Wharfe and turn right). Turn right along the river bank through wooded parkland to cross a suspension bridge over to the west bank. Continue beside the river, passing the miniature gorge of Loup Scar to the road bridge at Burnsall, emerging into the Main Street at the side of the Red Lion.

The church, originally built in the 12th century, was largely rebuilt in the 15th century.

Grassington
Upper Wharfedale's principle village has a medieval bridge, small cobbled market square and narrow streets. Grassington Moor, to the north, is covered with old lead mines which were worked in the late 18th and early 19th centuries. A National Park Centre provides a useful introduction to the Yorkshire Dales. Telephone: 0756 752774.

ℋEBDEN ~to~ ℬURNSALL

**APPROXIMATELY
3½ MILES**

*This is an easy walk
over high pastures to
Burnsall, returning
along a delightful path
beside the River
Wharfe.*

Parking
OS Map 98 Ref SE0262.
Hebden village, in the broad
street near the old school.

From the Post Office walk down Mill Lane, turning left onto the footpath next to the old school. Descend to the stream, cross the second footbridge and walk alongside the fish hatchery to the left. Shortly, turn left onto a path, waymarked Hartington Raikes, crossing a wall stile into pasture, then turn immediately right over a further wall stile and diagonally cross a field towards a farmhouse. Pass through the farmyard via two gates, then climb up through pasture to a stile in the field corner. Proceed along a track through the next pasture, following the right-hand wall to a ladder stile in the field corner. Cross the stile, keep to the wire fence and climb a further waymarked ladder stile, then follow the field edge round to a solitary tree, under which is a gated stile. Follow the field edge to a further wall stile, then follow the path downhill through a series of terraced fields, across a lane, continuing to the banks of the River Wharfe. Turn left for Burnsall and the pub.

☙*Red Lion (Free House)*☙

A pretty stone-built inn overlooking the river and village green. Good atmospheric pubby bar with panelled walls, oak benches, sturdy tables and chairs and woodburner, plus a comfortable lounge bar. Outside, there is a riverside terrace. Children are welcome and overnight accommodation is available.

On draught: Tetley Bitter, Theakston Best Bitter, Castlemaine XXXX, Skol, Carlsberg, Gaymers Olde English cider.

Food: the menu includes chicken liver pâté and Cumberland sauce (£2.75), steak and kidney pie (£5), poached salmon in white wine (£5.50), ploughman's (£4.75) and sandwiches (from £2.50). Puddings (£2.25). 3-course set dinner for £14.95.

Times: 12-2pm and 7-10pm. Open 11am-11pm (except Sun). Telephone: 0756 72204.

———◆◆◆◆———

On leaving the inn turn left, shortly to follow the riverbank path upstream, passing Loup Scar to the suspension bridge in ¾ mile. Cross the bridge, follow the path to the road and turn right to cross a small bridge over a stream. Take the footpath on the left, cross a stile and pass between two bungalows, eventually reaching the fish hatcheries passed on the outward route. Retrace your steps back to Hebden village.

Red Lion
Burnsall, Skipton - village centre on B6160, 3 miles south-west of Grassington.

FURTHER EXPLORATION

Bolton Abbey
The romantic ruins stand in parkland beside the River Wharfe, 3 miles south of Barden Bridge. The abbey was founded by Augustinian canons in 1151 and the nave survives in use to this day as a parish church.

Parcevall Hall Gardens, Skyreholme, near Appletreewick
In a beautiful hillside setting, east of the main Wharfedale valley, the gardens of this fine Elizabethan house are open daily Etr to Oct, and by appointment in winter. Telephone: 0756 720311.

ℋAWES ~to~ ℋARDRAW

**APPROXIMATELY
5½ MILES**

*A not-too-strenuous
walk through
riverbank meadows
before gaining higher
ground with views
across Wensleydale
and over the fells of
Cotterdale Common.*

Parking
OS Map 98 Ref MR8789. Gayle
Lane car park (charge) in
Hawes centre.

Green Dragon
Hardraw, Hawes. Off A64
2 miles north of Hawes.

FURTHER EXPLORATION

Hawes
Situated on the River Ure,
between two of England's
highest passes and near the
850ft head of Wensleydale,
Hawes is the commercial and
market centre for the area. A
market town since only 1700,
the High Street is lined with a
variety of stalls on Tuesdays.

From Gayle Lane, turn right along High Street, then opposite the Market House turn left between two houses on a well defined path, passing under a disused railway into pasture. Continue to the river, turn right along the bank and cross four ladder stiles and meadows to a footbridge across a stream and a road. Turn left, then shortly take the path left, waymarked Sedbusk. Cross a stile, a meadow and an arched footbridge, continuing uphill to cross a road via two stiles, then straight ahead, to join Sedbusk Lane. Turn right, then before the village, cross a stile on the left into pasture. Cross the meadow, turn left and join a track traversing several meadows and stiles to reach the road at Simonstone. Turn left and immediately right into the drive to Simonstone Hall, then before the entrance to the Hall, climb the stile, left into meadowland. At the farmhouse go through a gate and immediately turn left to go downhill to enter Hardraw, beside the Green Dragon.

⟫*Green Dragon (Theakston)*⟪

Access to the impressive waterfall of Hardraw Force is through this popular stone-built pub, once a coaching inn. There is a panelled public bar and a cosy, beamed snug bar with a coal fire. Traditional benches, tables and chairs furnish both bars. Children are welcome and overnight accommodation is available.

On draught: Theakston Best Bitter, XB and Old Peculier, Guinness, Harp, Carlsberg.
Food: generous bar meals include steak and chips (£4.25), steak pie (£4.45), ploughman's (£3.95), salads (from £3.95), filled jacket potatoes (from £1.95) and sandwiches (from £1.45).
Times: (bar meals) 12-2.30pm and 7-9pm. Pub open 11am-11pm. Telephone: 0969 667392.

On leaving the pub turn right and cross the bridge, then after passing the school house turn right onto a walled lane, signposted Pennine Way. Follow the lane for about a mile, then just to the north of a wood pass through the second gate in the wall to your left and follow the wall downhill to a gate at the bottom of a rough, rock strewn pasture. Continue downhill, shortly to follow the contour of the hill along an ill-defined yet waymarked path to a gate. Keep downhill, cross a stream and go through another gate into pasture and soon reach a road. Turn left, then immediately after crossing the bridge over Widdale Beck, turn right towards Appersett. Pass beneath Appersett railway viaduct, then turn left to follow the footpath to Ashes, climbing gently uphill over a stile into a meadow. Cross to the wall ahead, turn left to climb a ladder stile, then just beyond a gateway cross a stile and a stream and head uphill to a gate and track. Follow the track to a road and turn left back into Hawes.

Dales Countryside Museum, Hawes

Housed in the former railway station it features displays and an extensive collection of bygones and farming implements. Also here is a National Park and tourist information centre. Open Apr to Oct. Telephone: 0969 667450.

Hardraw Force

Set in a natural amphitheatre, Britain's highest single-drop waterfall cascades 100ft over a limestone edge into a deep pool and the adventurous can explore behind the fall. Access via the Green Dragon pub (charge).

Aysgarth ~to~ West Burton

**APPROXIMATELY
4½ MILES**

*An easy walk above
the banks of the River
Ure with glimpses of
some famous
Wensleydale
waterfalls, returning
through Bishopdale.*

Parking
OS Map 98 Ref MR0188.
Aysgarth Falls car park
(charge).

*L*eave the car park, turn right downhill to St Andrew's Church, and pass through the gates to follow the path through the churchyard to a stile. Cross meadowland, pass through a wood, then head across an open field to a tumbledown wall above the river. Follow the river downstream, eventually joining the river bank just below Lower Force waterfall. Continue beside the river through three pastures, via stiles, to reach the road at Hestholme Bridge. Turn left, then shortly after crossing the bridge over Walden Beck, turn right onto a footpath to Edgley. Pass through a small wood to a stile, then cross pasture to a gateway in its southern corner and a road. Turn right, then after 50 yards, left on a path, signed Flanders Hall, following the waymarked path across meadowland, passing an unusual cone-shaped folly on the left. Cross a stile into pasture then immediately after passing a small wood on your right, go through a gateway into a small

paddock. Pass a barn on the right, go through a gate, cross the next field and stile, then follow the path along the field edge over stiles to a lane. Turn right, cross the bridge over a beck and turn left along a raised pavement to the village green and pub.

⌀*Fox and Hounds* (Free House)⌀

The homely, whitewashed cottage overlooks the green in this idyllic Dales village. The single low-beamed bar is traditionally furnished and various prints and paintings, many of which are for sale, adorn the walls. Children are welcome. Bed and breakfast accommodation is available.

On draught: Black Sheep Bitter and Special, Websters Yorkshire Bitter, Younger's Scotch Bitter, Carlsberg, McEwan, Dry Blackthorn cider.

Food: home-cooked bar meals vary daily, but may include beef curry (£4.60), ploughman's (£3.50), giant Yorkshire puddings with assorted fillings (£2.50), beefburger and chips (£1.95)

Times: 12-1.45pm and 6.30-8.30pm. Telephone: 0969 663279.

On leaving the pub turn immediately left and follow the road for about 300 yards to a waymarked path between two houses. Cross a road, pass through a gate into pasture, then on entering a second meadow head towards the right-hand corner and the river bank. Turn right, and when you reach Eshington Lane, turn left and immediately after crossing a bridge cross a stile to climb through a series of meadows up to the A684. Cross over into the lane to St Andrew's Church. Enter the churchyard, turning left at the church to retrace your steps to the car park.

Fox and Hounds
West Burton, Leyburn. Just off B6160 Bishopdale to Wharfedale road.

FURTHER EXPLORATION

St Andrew's Church, Aysgarth
Largely rebuilt in 1866, it contains an elaborate rood screen dating from 1506 which, together with a magnificent carved vicar's stall, were removed from Jervaulx Abbey in 1536 after the Dissolution.

Yore Mill, Aysgarth
Built in 1784 on the banks of the River Ure below Aysgarth bridge, it was originally a corn mill and later a worsted woollen mill and flour mill. It houses the Yorkshire Carriage Museum, with over 60 vehicles. Open Apr - Oct and some winter weekends. Telephone: 0748 823275.

Aysgarth Falls
Confined by wooded banks, the River Ure falls over a series of broad, shallow terraces in a system extending over a mile. The Upper Falls, easily seen from the bridge and roadside have the most beautiful setting; the Middle and Lower Falls - the most dramatic - can be viewed by following a path through Freeholders' Wood.

$\mathcal{G}$OATHLAND ~to~ $\mathcal{B}$ECK HOLE

APPROXIMATELY 5 MILES

A pretty, easy going ramble through a varied landscape on field and riverside paths. The outward route is considerably longer than the return walk. Walkers may wish to take a picnic and lunch by the river, as the pub sells only sandwiches and snacks - or the Mallyan Spout Hotel does excellent meals and bar meals.

Parking
OS Map 94 Ref NZ8301. Car park opposite Post Office in Goathland village.

Birchall Inn
Beckhole, near Whitby. Off A169, two miles south of Grosmont.

FURTHER EXPLORATION
Goathland
An attractive village in the North York Moors National Park, some 500ft above sea level. The grey-stone buildings are set around a large village

From the car park turn left down the road, then just before Goathland Hotel, take the waymarked path (Goathland) on the right and keep left-handed through pasture (used as a campsite in summer), to a stile at the top of the field. Bear right across the next field, cross a stone bridge and keep left through the following two fields to another stile and path leading downhill to a gate and village road. Turn left, then right just before the attractive Mallyan Spout Hotel, onto a signposted path leading to the riverside. Turn left along the riverside path, signposted Mallyan Spout, pass the spectacular Mallyan Spout waterfall, continuing up river, crossing two bridges, and finally reaching a road. Turn right, then just beyond Julian Park Farm, take the arrowed footpath on your right to a wooden gate. Keep left-handed through the next field, descending to cross a stile into woodland. At a fork, follow the yellow arrow left, climb a stile and head downhill through a gate, then at a junction of paths follow the blue arrowed pathway straight down, keeping left. At the next signpost follow the yellow arrow right, signposted to Beck Hole. After the bridge, cross the stile immediately to your right and proceed to a gate and track that leads to Beck Hole. At the road, the pub lies slightly to your left.

∽*Birchall Inn (Free House)*∽

A timeless, rural gem of a pub idyllically placed beside a ghyll at the bottom of a green valley, this was originally two cottages dating back to 1600 and now combining the functions of pub, village shop and post office. The pretty, white-painted exterior has a unique landscape painting by Algernon Newton hanging from the wall. Children are welcome in the small family room and there is a garden.

On draught: Theakston Best Bitter, XB and Mild, Carlsberg Export, Strongbow cider.

green where a group of sword dancers, the Plough Stotts, regularly perform. The TV series, 'Heartbeat', is filmed in this area of extensive moorland and wooded valleys with lovely waterfalls, such as the 70ft Mallyan Spout, Thomason Foss, Nelly Ayre Foss and Water Ark.

Food: is limited to a few basic snacks like sandwiches, pies and sweets from the shop, available during opening hours - 11am-11pm Etr to Sep (except Sun), winter 12-3pm and 7.30-11pm. Telephone: 0947 86245.

North York Moors Railway, Pickering
Steam and diesel locomotives operate over 18 miles of track between Pickering and Grosmont, taking in some superb panoramic views along the way. The locomotive sheds at Pickering are open to the public. Telephone: 0751 73535.

From the pub, retrace your steps back down the track to the gate, then turn left to follow the wide path, signed Goathland. Continue through two kissing gates, cross a road and proceed on the well-defined path through a further two kissing gates to a road. Turn right to get back to your car.

OLD BYLAND~to~SCAWTON

APPROXIMATELY 5½ MILES

Undulating ramble across farmland and through wooded valleys, close to Ryedale and Rievaulx Abbey.

Parking
OS Map 100 Ref SE5485. Beside the village green in Old Byland.

Hare Inn
Scawton, near Helmsley. Village signposted off B1257 Helmsley to Stokesley road.

FURTHER EXPLORATION

Rievaulx Abbey
Magnificent in ruin, the impressive remains lie in the richly wooded valley of the River Rye. Walter L'Espec gave the site to the Cistercians in 1131 and this was the first church they built in the north of England. It was extremely prosperous and under its third abbot, Aelred (1147-67), there were 140 monks and over 500 lay brothers. By the time of the Dissolution there were only 12 monks left. Open all year. Telephone: 04396 228.

Walk down the village lane, then at the first right-hand bend, bear off left onto a path bearing left into the valley bottom. Keep left on a path along the valley floor as far as a T-junction with a track. Go steeply uphill, shortly follow bridleway signs through a farmyard, bearing round to the left to a gate and a pasture. Head straight across the field to another gate, turn right, then keep right-handed through the next field and pass through yet another gate to come to a small gate between a wall and a fence. Where the fence ends, turn almost 180 degrees left back round the other side of the fence down a track to the bottom of the hill. Leaving the lake to your left, head diagonally across a field to a wooden bridge. Cross, go through a gateway, then turn left through a kissing gate, and cross the next little bridge. Keep right, do not pass through the gate leading to a track, but head above and to the left of it up a steep bank, on a path that soon becomes distinct as it climbs to a road and a sharp bend. Go straight on into Scawton, and the pub is at the top of the village.

☙*Hare Inn* (Free House)❧

A pretty, white-painted cottage tracing its history back to 1153 when monks from Old Byland first built a hostel for travellers using the old road to Old Byland and Rievaulx Abbeys. A warm welcome awaits walkers in the simply furnished, cosy bar.

On draught: Younger's Scotch Bitter, Theakston Best Bitter, XB and Old Peculier, Gillespies Malt Stout, Harp, McEwan, Scrumpy Jack cider.

Food: a changing menu may offer duck-liver pâté with port (£2.50), seafood lasagne, roast lamb with orange and mint tartlets and spicy lentil pie (all at £4.95). Puddings (£2.50). Traditional Sunday roast.

Times: 12-2pm, 6.30 (7 winter)-9.30pm Closed Mon lunchtime. Telephone: 0845 597289.

From the pub turn right, shortly take the waymarked path left beside the telephone box. Cross the stile, bear left over pasture to a gate, then cross straight over the next field to another gate, then join a track bearing right around woodland and up a small embankment. Cross a field, keeping to the right, then maintain direction across two stiles, a small field and keep to the left of subsequent fields, climbing many stiles until you cross the centre of a field to a final stile into woodland. Bear left downhill to a T-junction of paths, turn right and descend to the woodland edge where the path joins a track. Turn right, then at a path intersection (crossed on your outward journey), turn left over a stile to cross a field, a wooden bridge, then climb a steep, wooded hillside to a gate at the top. Keep right-handed through two fields via gates, cross over a track, through another gate, then into a bushy, wooded area and down into a hallow valley. Climb the other side to a small wicket gate and the village road. Turn right to get back into the village.

Rievaulx Terraces and Temples

This curved, grassy terrace, half a mile long, looks down onto the abbey and beyond over Ryedale. It has two mock temples and remarkablefrescoes by Borgnis. (National Trust) Open Apr - Oct. Telephone: 04396 340.

ℛOSEDALE ABBEY 𝒸IRCULAR 𝓌ALK

APPROXIMATELY 4 MILES

A very scenic and gently undulating rural walk through pleasant Rosedale countryside

Parking

OS Maps 94 or 100 Ref SE7197. Two car parks in the village.

From the Milburn Arms turn right, go straight over a crossroads, leaving the village green to your left to follow the road past the school. Shortly, take the waymarked footpath, left, soon to turn right along a campsite road past a playground on your left. Follow footpath signs past various camping fields to a kissing gate, then cross two fields to a stile and enter a wooded area. Take the second path left down to another path beside the river and follow signs across fields to a stile leading to a rough track. Turn left here, cross a dilapidated gate and go straight over a field (ignore the bridge on the left), then at a path intersection, near a telegraph pole, bear diagonally right across the field, over a stile and small bridge, then straight across the next two fields via kissing gates, and follow a rough track left, uphill through a gate to Hill Cottages. From the phone box, head uphill to the track on the right through the gate, waymarked Plaxton. Just before a ramshackle farm building, bear right through a gate onto a track downhill to a house. Turn left behind the house over a stile, then bear left uphill to a T-junction of paths at the top. Turn right, shortly cross two stiles and turn right along a lane, shortly to take the path signed left and soon turn right at a gate and disused house. Beyond a pond, bear half-left down a field to a gap in the wall and maintain direction to a ladder stile , then beyond a gap in another wall turn left along a lane. Shortly, turn right at a fingerpost and walk parallel to a stream, eventually dropping down to cross a bridge. Follow the bridleway sign up a small hill and across pasture to a bridge over a stream, then head straight across the next field to a gate and bear right to a ladder stile. A path (yellow arrows) follows the stream towards Rosedale, then just outside the village at a gate and fork of paths, keep straight ahead to another gate and the car park to the Milburn Arms.

⊷*Milburn Arms* (Free House)⊷

Largely built in the mid-1700s with a few more recent additions, this attractive York-stone hotel has a spacious pubby bar with low beams and traditional furniture. There is also a smart, split-level restaurant and a pleasant walled garden, with tables set beneath a cedar tree. Children are welcome. The inn has 11 bedrooms.

On draught: Bass, Worthington Best Bitter, Theakston Old Peculier, guest ale, Guinness, Carling Black Label, Carlsberg.
Food: bar meals include starters like local sausages with venison and onion gravy and tiger fish prawns in garlic butter (both £2.95), followed by pan-fried supreme of salmon (£4.95), grilled Farndale goat's cheese and salad (£5.25) or beef and Guinness casserole (£5.45). Desserts (£1.95) include sticky toffee pudding and summer pudding.
Times: 12-2pm and 7-9.30pm (10pm Sat).
Telephone: 07515 312.

Milburn Arms
Rosedale Abbey, Pickering. Village off A170 west of Pickering.

FURTHER EXPLORATION

Rosedale
This long and scenic valley is watered by the River Seven, fed by moorland streams. To the east are the conifers of Cropton Forest, and splendid moors, steep hills and outstanding views surround the dale. Rosedale Abbey is the largest community in the valley, but of the priory founded here in 1158, only the short tower and staircase remain.

ℋOLE OF HORCUM ~to~ ℒEVISHAM

*A splendid ramble
across open moorland
on clear paths with
good views, returning
along an undulating
path through a
wooded valley*

Parking
OS Map 94 or 100 Ref SE8593.
Hole of Horcum car park on
Pickering/Whitby road, A169.

Horseshoe Inn
Levisham, Pickering. Off A169
Pickering to Whitby road,
signed Lockton and Levisham

**FURTHER EXPLORATION
Levisham**
Set high on open moorland, the
village consists of a typical
North Riding main street, with
a wide lawn to the left and
right. The lane by the left hand
side of the pub leads downhill
to Levisham Station, on the
North York Moors Steam
Railway from Pickering to
Grosmont.

From the car park, cross the road and follow the roadside path right. At the path intersection where the road banks steeply right, take the waymarked middle track straight ahead (Link pathway) and keep to this path past a small pond and over spectacular moorland. Eventually, you descend to a junction of paths by another small pond, and follow the one signed Levisham which bears slightly left and passes through a gate onto a track which becomes a lane as you come down into the village beside the pub.

⊸Horseshoe Inn *(Free House)*⊸

This traditional stone-built pub dating back to the 16th century has modernised its bars, which are now spacious and comfortable. It stands at the head of the wide village street, lined on both sides by farmhouses and cottages, and there is seating outside on the green. Children are welcome.

On draught: Theakston Best Bitter, XB and Old Peculier, Tetley Bitter, Harp, Beck's Bier.
Food: the menu may feature devilled whitebait (£2.75) steak and kidney pie (£4.50), fresh local trout (£5.50) and a selection of vegetarian dishes. Puddings include cheesecake and treacle sponge (both £2.25).
Times: 12-2pm and 7-9pm. Telephone: 0751 60240.

From the pub walk to the end of the village street then where the road bends right downhill out of the village, take the waymarked path on the left. Keep to this path, following signs to Saltergate and eventually cross two small bridges in the valley bottom and bear left. Climb a stile, continue straight across the centre of pasture to join a rough, little-used track. Pass to the right of an old house, then bear slightly downhill to a stile and continue with the arrow, your defined path ascending back to the A169. At the top follow the roadside path back to the car park.

*R*YDAL ~to~ *G*RASMERE

**APPROXIMATELY
5 MILES**

*This is a varied and
scenic walk, full of
interest and history
being in the very heart
of literary Lakeland. It
ranges from the gentle
and grassy to the
more strenuous and
rocky.*

Parking
OS Map 90 Ref NY3606,
Peterbridge car park.

Lamb Inn
Grasmere. The village is just
off A591 between Ambleside
and Keswick.

FURTHER EXPLORATION

**Dove Cottage and The
Wordsworth Museum,
Grasmere**
Wordsworth called Grasmere
'the loveliest spot that man
hath found'. He lived at Dove
Cottage from 1799 to 1808 and
wrote much of his best-known
poetry here. Telephone 05394
35544 & 35547.

Rydal Mount, Rydal
Wordsworth's home from 1813
until his death in 1850.
Telephone: 05394 33002.

From car park, tun left along road for about ¼ mile
to a defined track on left. Enter Rydal Woods and
bear right towards Rydal Water. Shortly, leave
lakeside to follow wall along lower slopes of
Loughrigg Terrace. Follow slate sign set in wall for
'Grasmere, High Close and Langdale' and soon
descend towards weir at the southern end of Grasmere.
Continue through woodland on the lake shore to a
sharp left-hand turn and join lane. Turn right, then at
T-junction facing the church, turn left into the village
for the Lamb Inn.

❧ *Lamb Inn* (Free House) ❧

Although part of the Red Lion Hotel, the stone-fronted
Lamb is an ideal place for a pint of real ale and a bar
meal after a day of effort on the fells. Wood and stone
characterise the comfortable interior. Children
welcome in the Buttery.

On draught: Theakston Best and XB, Younger's Scotch,
Guinness, McEwan, Carlsberg Export, Coors Extra
Gold, Dry Blackthorn cider.

Food: choices include sandwiches, a wide variety of
pizzas (£4), the 'ultimate Yorkshire pudding' (£3-£5),
Cumberland sausage, gammon steak, fillet of cod and
halibut (£4-£6)

Times: 12-2.30pm (2pm Sun) and 6.30-9pm (7pm Sun).
Telephone: 05394 35456.

Return through the village, passing church, and
car park to the A591.Cross onto lane towards
Dove Cottage, ascend and bear sharp right by Rydal
signpost. Lane eventually peters out to become a stony
footpath along the lower edge of Heron Pike and Nab
Scar.Continue through trees and across open fields to
the rear of Rydal Mount to a road. Turn right downhill
and rejoin A591. Turn left, then shortly cross narrow
hump-backed bridge on right back to the car park.

𝒟ENTDALE ~ 𝑅AMBLE

*A delightful ramble
through Dentdale,
often beside the River
Dee with its small
attractive waterfalls
and rapids. Numerous
stiles and gates have
to be negotiated as
you pass from farm to
farm.*

Parking
OS Map 98 Ref SD7486. Car park on the north side of the river by the signpost to Nelly Bridge.

Sun Inn
Main Street, Dent. Village signposted of A164 in Sedbergh

FURTHER EXPLORATION

St Andrew's Church, Dent
Built in late-Perpendicular style, the church contains a fine three-decker pulpit dating from 1614.

From the car park, facing the river Dee take the footpath in the right-hand corner, to the waterfalls. Shortly, rejoin the lane towards Dent, then in about ¾ mile, turn right beside a white cottage towards Cross House. Take the double track on the left behind the house, pass through a gate, then, at some farm buildings, keep them on your right and cross the top corner of a pasture. Cross straight over several fields, following yellow marks (some faint) on gates and walls. On the way, you will cross a stream via a stone slab bridge, skirt a fenced plantation, and cross a wooden bridge by Gillside Cottages. Beyond the cottages and more fields, where a farm road bends left towards the road below, look for a gate in the hedge on your right and cross fields on the waymarked path with Dent in view to your left. Eventually, at a whitewashed cottage, go left down the farm track to the road. Turn left and shortly right to join a path to Church Bridge. Cross the field and enter Dent, going past the church to the Sun Inn.

☙ *Sun Inn* (Dent Brewery) ☙

Tucked down a cobbled street this whitewashed stone pub, once a smithy, dates back to 1640. Inside, three small, cosy rooms (one no smoking) radiate from the central bar. At the rear a converted barn houses a tiny brewery. Children are welcome, as are dogs. Guest bedrooms are available.

On draught: Dent Bitter, Ramsbottom Strong Ale and T'owd Tup, Younger's Scotch, Guinness.

Food: freshly cooked and generously served dishes include home-made beefburger, onion and chips (£2.70), chicken curry (£3.25), Cumberland sausages (£3.75), rump steak (£4.95) and a cold table featuring salads - beef (£4.15) - and a range of sandwiches (from £1.45). Children's helpings (£1.75).

Times: 12-2pm and 6.30-8pm (7-8.30pm in winter), bar open 11am-11pm in summer. Telephone: 05396 25208.

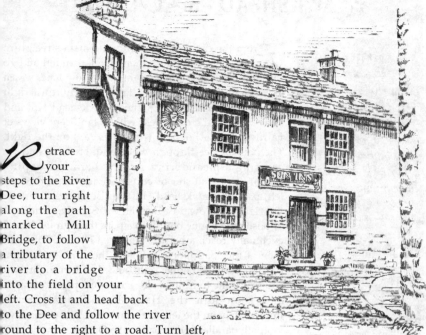

*R*etrace your steps to the River Dee, turn right along the path marked Mill Bridge, to follow a tributary of the river to a bridge into the field on your left. Cross it and head back to the Dee and follow the river round to the right to a road. Turn left, climb gently uphill with woods on your right and pass a Methodist Church, Smithy Fold and Whernside Manor. Just beyond Syke Fold take the marked path on your right to Ewegales Bridge. Cross the corner of the field to the high stone wall stile, turn left and follow yellow signs to the white house ahead, your path crossing its front garden and passing to the rear of the stone cottage next door, before climbing uphill into pasture. Pass behind the next big house ahead and pick up footpath signs to another farm. As the road beyond the farm sweeps left look for the signpost in the corner, right, directing you to Clint. Keep right-handed through pasture towards a large grey house, where the path bears diagonally left across its front and proceeds to the next farm. Turn left down to the lane, turn right, then in 100 yards take the path, left, signposted Nelly Bridge. Cross the field and the bridge and walk back up to the car park.

Dent's History

In the 17th and 18th centuries Dent was famous for its knitting industry and first-floor spinning galleries were a feature of the houses that line its delightful cobbled streets.

ℋAWKSHEAD ~to~ 𝒪UTGATE

From the car park, walk into the main street, turn right, then at the Red Lion Hotel, turn left and go through the archway ahead into a narrow lane, which slowly climbs out of the village. Shortly, turn right onto a waymarked path signed Hawkshead Hill and Tarn Hows and cross a field with magnificent views of Fairfield Horseshoe and Kirkstone Pass on the right. The path passes through woodland, crossing and re-crossing a meandering stream, before dropping downhill to a cluster of cottages and the road. Turn left, passing Hawkshead Hill Baptist Chapel and take the right fork towards Tarn Hows. Shortly, turn right opposite the phone box, onto a path through fields and eventually reach a narrow lane by a hamlet. Turn left, then at the road junction follow the Ambleside sign, passing Borwick Lodge, right, and then turn right onto a narrow lane to Knipe Fold. Pass some pretty cottages and soon join the Hawkshead-Outgate road. Immediately on the left, at the junction, is a permissive footpath parallel to the road to the Outgate Inn.

Turn right on leaving the inn and in 30 yards, by Rose Cottage, take the footpath on your right, signposted Stevney. The field ahead falls away sharply to a stone slab bridge over a stream at the bottom. Look then for a ladder stile over a high wall on the right and follow the arrows towards the farm building up the hill. From here there are good views of Bletham Tarn and the top end of Windermere. The footpath turns sharp right, right again by a National Trust sign for Hawkshead, then a succession of marker posts leads across fields to a farm, where you turn left into the lane and then immediately right again towards Hawkshead which can now be seen clearly ahead. White marker posts indicate your route through fields to a narrow lane where you turn left, then in 50 yards turn right through a gate to follow the path diagonally across a field and over a bridge into Hawkshead.

∽*Outgate Inn (Hartleys)*∾

A very popular, friendly 18th-century rural inn with genuine low beams, wooden tables and chairs throughout the three inter-connecting rooms. which give it a real atmosphere. Various books and nick-nacks on shelves and local photographs decorate the walls. It appeals to traditional jazz fans, with bands playing every Friday night. Children are welcome in the dining area, but not after 9pm. Dogs are welcome in one part of the bar.

On draught: Hartleys XB, Robinson's Best Bitter, Castlemaine XXXX, Tennants Extra, Strongbow cider. Food: mostly home-made fare includes smoked salmon pâté, mussels provençal, herrings in sour cream (£2.95), Outgate grill (£5.75), Esthwaite rainbow trout (£6.25), smoked-pork loin steaks (£5.25), vegetarian dishes (£5.25) and a range of freshly-cut sandwiches (£1.50-£4.75). Puddings (£1.50-£2) and children's meals (from £2.25).
Times: 12-2pm and 6.30-9pm (Sun from 7pm). Telephone: 05394 36413.

Beatrix Potter Gallery, Main Street
The gallery has an award-winning exhibition of selected original Beatrix Potter drawings and illustrations from her children's books.
Telephone: 05394 36355.

Grizedale Forest Visitor Centre, Grizedale
The centre illustrates the story of the forest. There are various trails, a children's play area and picnic sites. Telephone: 0229 860010

AROUND LAKE BUTTERMERE

**APPROXIMATELY
4 MILES**

*A not-too-strenuous
walk, affording
magnificent views,
around picturesque
Buttermere, set in a
bowl of mountains.*

Parking
OS Map 89 Ref NY1959,
Gatesgarth car park.

Bridge Hotel
Buttermere. On B5289 south of
Cockermouth.

FURTHER EXPLORATION

Buttermere Valley
The Buttermere Valley is one
of Britain's loveliest with
renowned fells such as Red
Pike, High Stile, High Crag and
Haystacks dominating
Buttermere, Crummock Water
and Loweswater. The whole
area offers superb walking.

*T*ake the footpath opposite the car park through
fields towards the southern end of the lake. On
reaching the far shore turn right along the bridleway,
signposted Buttermere. It follows the shoreline, then
where it heads into woodland, bear right on a footpath
along the shore, eventually rejoining the bridleway at
the top end of the lake. Continue through fields to the
Bridge Hotel, which can be seen clearly ahead.

Bridge Hotel (Free House)

The building boasts an ancient history and every
period has added its own mark to this comfortable
hotel. Two friendly bars have low oak beams and
cushioned chairs and there is also a patio with superb
views. Children, but not dogs, are welcome inside.

On draught: Theakston Best, XB and Old Peculier,
Younger's No.3, Black Sheep Best, McEwan 80/-,
Guinness and Weston Old Rosie cider. Also available
are a good selection of wines and malt whiskies.
Food: well prepared meals include local dishes like
spicy Cumberland sausage (£5.20), Cumberland hotpot
(£4.95) and poached Borrowdale trout (£6). A walkers'
snack corner at lunchtimes only features pâtés,
ploughman's, salads and open sandwiches (around
£3.50). There is also a vegetarian menu (£4.40-£5.20).
Times: (food) 9-10am (breakfast), 12-2.30pm, 3-5.30pm
(afternoon tea) and 6-9.30pm; (bar) 11am-11pm.
Telephone: 07687 70252.

*L*eave the hotel and turn right onto the road
climbing steeply towards the church. At Syke
Farm take the waymarked bridleway, right, towards
the lake shore. The path skirts the shore, goes through
a short tunnel, passes a shingle beach close to the end
of the lake, before merging with the road. Follow the
road for a few hundred yards back to the car park.

*W*ATEREND~to~*L*OWESWATER

*W*ith the lake on your right follow the road towards Loweswater village, then at the end of the stone wall enclosing farmland, turn right onto a narrow track towards the lake. Follow the lake shore for some distance before rejoining the road. Pass, on left, Crabtree Beck cottages, then, right, a bridleway, (your return path) and proceed past the road arrowed to Buttermere. At the next junction turn right by Loweswater school, and walk down to the inn, enjoying a view of the north end of Crummock Water.

Kirkstile Inn (Free House)

This quaint black-and-white timbered inn dates from the 16th century. Its low-beamed rooms, open fires, wooden tables, settles and pub games have kept a traditional atmosphere where walkers are warmly welcomed, as are children and dogs. The inn has guest bedrooms and a pleasant garden.

On draught: Jennings Bitter, Younger's Scotch, Guinness, McEwan Export, Strongbow cider.

Food: includes filled rolls, open sandwiches (£1.75-£4.35), ploughman's, omelettes (£4.60), Cumberland sausage, egg and chips (£4.75) and specials like bacon and tomato casserole (£4.50).

Times: (bar) 11am-11pm; (food) 12-2.30pm and 6-9pm (7pm Sun); Telephone: 0900 85219

*R*etrace your steps to the bridleway (mentioned on outward route), which leads to the lake. Pass an NT car park, then on approaching Watergate Farm, cut across the field corner to a gate into Holme Wood and join a lakeside track. Where the path divides, one fork leads through the wood, the other, to your right, skirts the shore. Eventually they merge again to cross farmland to Hudson Place Farm. Pass through the farm, follow a road downhill. At a sharp left bend turn right onto a footpath, cross fields, a marshy area and two stiles back to Waterend.

APPROXIMATELY 4 MILES

A fairly gentle walk along both shores of Loweswater, with magnificent views of Melbreak, towering above Loweswater village and the hills round Crummock Water.

Parking
OS Map 89 Ref NY1122. Lay-by beside the phone box on the lakeside road near Waterend or ¼ mile along the lane towards Loweswater.

Kirkstile Inn
Loweswater, Cockermouth. The village is ½ miles off B5289, south of Cockermouth.

TOCKHOLES CIRCULAR WALK

APPROXIMATELY 4 MILES

A farmland stroll encompassing some fine views and a little Lancashire history.

Parking
OS Map 103 Ref SD6623.
Roddlesworth
Information Centre, adjacent to
the Royal Arms, Tockholes
Road, Tockholes.

The Rock
Tockholes - village signposted
off A666 south of Blackburn.

FURTHER EXPLORATION

Darwen Tower
Looking like a space rocket,
this tower can be seen for
most of the walk. It was built
to commemorate Queen
Victoria's Diamond Jubilee.
There are superb views from
the top.

Take the footpath opposite the Royal Arms, and shortly join the main track that bears right through the woods. At a junction of paths keep ahead to the end of Upper Roddlesworth Reservoir, then follow the path round to the left and beside the stream before crossing a stone slab bridge. Shortly, turn right to follow a woodland path to the other end of the reservoir, where you first see Darwen Tower in the distance. Bear right into a hollow below the wall of the reservoir turning left at the other side to head up into woodland. Just beyond a junction where a path converges from the right, bear off right to join a narrow track through the shrubbery to a kissing gate and pasture. Head for Higher Hill Farm on the skyline and cross the farm drive into a further field, then follow the wall left-handed to a kissing gate in the bottom corner. Keep straight ahead across a wall stile into a small field and pass through the gate in the left-hand corner to turn right along a narrow lane. Pass what were once weavers' cottages on your left, then in Chapels Lane pass more cottages and Tockholes United Reform Church. Continue ahead at the road junction for the Rock Inn which you will see to the right at the top of the hill.

Turn right on leaving the inn to follow the main road for 300 yards, before turning left into Weasel Lane. Just beyond where the unmetalled track veers sharp right, turn left by a black and white house and soon see Earnsdale Reservoir to your right. Go through a farm gate, turn sharp right along the narrow road and on reaching the reservoir turn right again up a narrow, stony track. Look out for a small gate in the wall on your left, then cross fields heading for the buildings on the skyline. Pass through a farm and between two private houses back to the car park.

⤳*The Rock* (Thwaites)⤳

This old Lancashire pub was 'modernised' as long ago as 1791, but actually traces its history back to the 10th century and is reputed to be haunted. The cosy two-roomed bar is comfortably furnished and decorated with various brasses, old plates and sporting prints. Outside, there is a small terrace which affords far-reaching views across wooded pastures to the coast, some 20 miles away. Children are welcome and dogs can be housed in the inn's own kennels.

On draught: Thwaites Best Bitter, Mild, Carlsberg, Carling Black Label, Strongbow cider.
Food: well priced, home-made dishes include beef in ale (£4.95), steak pie (£3.75), swordfish steak (£5.75), chicken baked in wine (£4.95) and a selection of sandwiches (from £1.35).
Times: 12-2pm and 7-10pm, (except Mon), all day Sun 12-8.50pm. Closed Mon lunch. Telephone: 0254 702733.

Tockholes
Hidden in Tockholes woods are the ruins of Hollinshead Hall. Nearby, a stream tumbles out of a lion's mouth at the restored Well House. The site is one of ancient habitation and even when the winds are howling off the moors people say it is always quiet and peaceful here.

ℰ AVES WOOD ~to~ 𝒴EALAND CONYERS

**APPROXIMATELY
5½ MILES**

*A walk mainly
through farmland and
woodland, but
encompassing the
grounds of a neo-
gothic mansion and a
nature reserve, with
occasional views of
the Cumbrian Fells
and Morecambe Bay.*

Parking
OS Map 97 Ref SD4776.
National Trust car park at
Eaves Wood.

New Inn
Yealand Conyers - village
signed off A6 and is 3 miles
from M6, junction 35.

FURTHER EXPLORATION

**Leighton Moss Nature
Reserve (RSPB)**
Includes Britain's largest
concentration of bitterns, as
well as otters and red and roe
deer.

From the car park turn left, then immediately right up the road, turning left at some cottages into Moss Lane. On reaching a row of grey stone houses at right angles to the lane, take the waymarked path opposite through a gap in the wall and follow the yellow arrows on telegraph poles and trees in woodland until you arrive at a small clearing near the top of the wood. Climb a stile in the top left-hand corner, then keep left-handed across two fields to a wall stile near the field corner. Turn right onto a well defined path through woodland, then where your path curves to the left bear off right onto a narrow track through shrubs to a gate. Continue along the established path through a wooded area in which there are plenty of examples of the limestone pavements, for which the area is renowned. Eventually, on arriving at a road and a three-way junction, proceed ahead along the Yealand Redmayne road, shortly to turn right at a footpath waymarker into Cringlebarrow Wood. Head deep into the woods until the path forks by a fenced field. Climb the stile into the field, keep left-handed until the path re-enters the wood, then turn immediately right onto a narrow track and follow it through the wood into Yealand Conyers and to the pub.

⊶*New Inn (Hartleys)*⊷

Low ceilings, exposed beams and a delightfully unspoilt traditional atmosphere are features of this welcoming ivy-clad pub with its tiny public bar and cottagey dining room. The building dates back to 1600. Various tools adorn the walls and a good fire warm the bar in winter. The sheltered rear garden is filled with roses and shrubs. Children of all ages are welcome in the dining room at lunchtime, but only those over 14 years old in the evening.

On draught: Hartleys XB, Robinson's Best Bitter, Guinness.

Food: the bar menu ranges from ploughman's, salads (£3.95-£5.50) and sandwiches (from £1.40) to steak and kidney pie (£3.75), prawns and mussels in a tangy sauce (£3.75), rack of lamb (£6.75) and trout (£6.15). In the evenings there is a separate dining room menu.
Times: 11.30am (12 Sun)-1.45pm and 6 (7 Sun)-8.45pm.
Telephone: 0524 723938.

Leighton Hall
A neo-Gothic mansion displaying, among other treasures, early Gillow furniture. Large collection of birds of prey, some of which can be seen flying each afternoon. Telephone: 0524 734474.

From the inn, turn left up hill, passing the Quaker Meeting House, then at a road junction and the Leighton Hall sign turn right. Where the road bends sharp left, bear off right through a gap in the wall into pasture to follow the yellow footpath markers uphill and across an open field until you see Leighton Hall and Leighton Moss below. Descend towards the Hall, soon to pass between it and the tennis courts. The road winds through farmland passing through Grisedale Farm before turning right to the causeway across Leighton Moss. Beyond the causeway, turn right onto the road, then in 100 yards turn left onto a path, signposted Red Bridge Lane. Cross the centre of the field to the bottom left-hand corner and then cross a further field to enter woodland. Proceed along a track that bears left through old quarry workings towards a metal gate. Fifty yards before the gate, bear left with a narrow shrub-edged track to the railway. Cross the railway line via two stiles, emerge from the wood and turn immediately right to join Moss Lane and proceed back to Eaves Wood car park.

$\mathcal{C}$OLLIER WOOD ~to~ $\mathcal{F}$IR TREE

APPROXIMATELY 4½ MILES

A rural walk through rolling countryside with many farm animals and only one significant climb. Some parts can be muddy, so stout footwear is advisable.

Parking

OS Map 92 Ref NZ1336. Collier Wood picnic area and car park.

$\mathcal{F}$rom the car-park entrance, turn right onto a bridleway, pass through a gate, and where the track turns right to a farm, keep straight on through another gate and go down to the road. Turn right, and shortly cross to a waymarked gate and head straight across pasture to a gate on the left of a clump of trees. With woodland to your right cross pasture and pass through two more gates, then at a farm drive, turn sharp left through a gate. Follow the track over a field to a stile by a gate, pass a silver birch coppice to another gate, and where the track bears left, continue straight across pasture. Go through a gate, bear slightly right, towards the bottom corner of woodland, cross a stream, go through a narrow gate and diagonally left uphill towards a clump of trees. Pass through a metal gate, then keeping trees on your left, pass through two metal gates and descend to a farmhouse. Keep it to your right and go through a gate onto the drive, then turn right and just beyond buildings go through the green gate in the fence on your left and head diagonally across a field to another gate. Keeping hedge and woods to your right, cross pasture to a white gate in the right-hand corner and continue uphill to a concrete road. Turn left, then left again at the main road and left at the crossroads. After about 100 yards turn right and cross to the pub.

⟡*Duke of York Inn* (Free House)⟡

Built in 1749 to serve drovers and coaches plying between England and Scotland, this attractive whitewashed inn is set in large gardens. Inside, the three welcoming rooms are comfortably furnished. Children are welcome anywhere in the pub.

On draught: Bass, Stones Best Bitter, Guinness, Tennents Pilsner, Carling Black Label, and an extensive list of wines.

Food: reliable dishes range from chicken Marengo, gammon in sherry and peach sauce, ham in Cumberland sauce, steak and kidney pie and beef stroganoff, to assorted salads and open sandwiches. The restaurant has a separate menu and there is a traditional Sunday lunch.

Times: (food) 11am-2pm and 6-10pm; (bar) 10am-11pm in summer with afternoon teas. Telephone: 0388 762848.

*R*etrace your steps back to the crossroads, turn left to join a metalled track between terraced houses which winds its way up and over the hill to a main road. Turn left, then after 100 yards cross the road and go through a gate with a conifer wood on your left. Traverse two fields and turn left keeping the hedge to your right all the way to a gate in the top right-hand corner. Join an old road, walk past a bench and keep on to a T-junction. Turn right here, eventually reaching a junction with buildings on the right and a private road straight on. Turn left and follow the road until it joins the main road. Cross over and you will see Collier Wood picnic area ahead.

Duke of York Inn
Fir Tree, near Crook. On A68.

FURTHER EXPLORATION

Raby Castle, Staindrop (off A688 to the south)
Stronghold of the Nevill and later the Vane families, Raby is one of the great castles of England. The present building is mostly 14th-century. It has nine towers, a medieval hall and kitchen and houses fine collections inside. It is set in gardens and a 200-acre deer park. Telephone: 0833 60202.

Escomb
(south off A689)
One of the best preserved Saxon churches in England, Escomb dates from the 7th century.

*E*DMUNDBYERS ~to~ *C*ARTERWAY HEADS

APPROXIMATELY 6 MILES

This attractive and varied walk takes in moorland, country lanes and the Derwent Reservoir.

Start of walk

OS Map 87 Ref NZ1651. Edmundbyers village.

Manor House Inn

Carterway Heads, near Shotley Bridge. On A68, just north of B6278, near Derwent Reservoir.

*T*ake the footpath beside the YMCA Hostel at the east end of the village on B6278, go through a gate, down a short drive and through a second gate, keeping the caravan site on your right. Descend into a valley with Burnhope Burn at the bottom and cross a wooden bridge. Turn left, follow the burn for a short distance and cross a small stream coming in from your right. Follow this stream uphill through some trees. The path soon bears slightly left and then zig-zags uphill to a fence with a stile. Climb over, turn immediately left, and follow the path to where it divides just before a group of silver birch trees. Keep right, then as you emerge from the trees, head across the field, aiming for the telegraph pole on the far side and cross the wall stile to its right. Proceed up the field to a metal gate and road. Turn right, then almost immediately turn left onto a track that bears left and slowly climbs up across the moor. Eventually, where the track forks, take the right-hand route and keep climbing steadily. At the top of the climb (good views) the track divides again, and this time keep left to follow the track across the top of the moor for about a mile, before descending to a road by a group of trees and a

house called Key West. Turn left, follow the road for ¾ mile, then at a T-junction keep ahead over a cattle grid and continue down this road for a further ¾ mile, crossing the River Derwent and eventually reaching the B6278. Turn right, then take the next left and gently climb up to the Manor House Inn.

⌘*Manor House Inn* (Free House)⌘

This splendid stone-built pub, dating from 1860, enjoys an isolated position high on the moors overlooking Derwent Reservoir and the hills beyond. A comfortable relaxed atmosphere prevails throughout the refurbished lounge bar and beamed public bar, which is furnished in traditional style.The excellent seating outdoors offers stunning views over moorland. Children are welcome in the eating areas until 9pm.

On draught: Butterknowle Bitter, McEwan's Scotch Bitter, Centurion Bitter, guest ales, Beamish, Fosters, Carlsberg, Stowford Press cider. Good range of wines and country wines.

Food: wide selection of good, imaginative food changes frequently and may include pork stroganoff (£5.85), baked sea trout in mint butter (£6.75), pasta gratin with tomatoes and basil (£4.50), lamb and aubergine casserole or roast pepper and red onion tart. Puddings range from plum and almond tart to treacle sponge (from £2).There is also a table d'hôte 3-course menu (£15).

Times: 12-2.30pm and 7-9.30pm (9pm Sun). Telephone: 0207 55268.

After leaving the inn, retrace your steps down the hill and turn right on to the B6278. Continue on this road until you reach the entrance to Derwent Reservoir. Turn right onto the reservoir road, cross the cattle grid and follow the road uphill until you reach the top of the dam. Keeping to the road, cross the dam with its beautiful views and follow the road as it begins to turn to the left, eventually bringing you back to a T-junction with the B6278. Turn right and after a short walk arrive back at the village of Edmundbyers.

FURTHER EXPLORATION

Edmundbyers
The village houses are scattered around large greens near the Church of St Edmunds, which has some very interesting woodwork acquired from churches around the country. Nearby Derwent Reservoir, 3½ miles long, is the largest stretch of fresh water in the area and is popular with yachtsmen and anglers. Pow Hill Country Park surrounds the reservoir and there are good areas for picnics.

Blanchland
This small, isolated village is thought to be named after the white habits of Premonstratensian monks who settled there in the 12th century. The present church was built in 1752 using those parts of the old abbey church which had survived. There are three fine medieval tombstones on the transept floor, and many interesting artefacts.

ℒOGGERHEADS COUNTRY PARK ~to~ 𝒞ILCAIN

**APPROXIMATELY
6¼ MILES**

*An enjoyable walk
across farmland with
fine mountain
scenery, returning
along the spectacular
Leete Path noted for
its gorges, cliff faces
and caves.*

Parking
OS Map 116 Ref SJ 1962.
Loggerheads Country Park off
A494, 3 miles from Mold

White Horse
Cilcain, Mold. Village
signposted from A494 west of
Mold.

FURTHER EXPLORATION

**Loggerheads Country
Park**
Attractions include a craft
shop, an information centre, a
200-year-old flour and saw
mill, an exhibition centre and a
restaurant. Towering over it
are 320 million-year-old
carboniferous limestone cliffs
which can be reached by
exploring the many nature
trails.

From the main entrance turn sharp right up the narrow lane overlooking Loggerheads. At a crossroads turn right signposted Cilcain, then in 20 yards by a large house, take the waymarked footpath left into farmland, with a stream on your right and Ffrith Mountain immediately to your left. Follow waymarker posts to Moel Famau. One post (hidden behind tree on woodland edge) directs you right into pasture, across a second field, then in the bottom corner bear right with blue arrow. Soon follow sign to Cilcain leading to a narrow country lane, then shortly branch off left by some newly renovated cottages onto a lane which affords fine valley views. Eventually Cilcain church comes into view and keep to this almost straight path, ignoring paths left uphill, your route curving sharp right as you descend towards Cilcain. At the bottom turn right, then left into the village to a crossroads by the church, the pub lies to the right.

✎ *White Horse Inn* (Free House) ✎

Dating from the 14th century, this delightful creeper-clad and flower-decked village inn has a cosy, low beamed interior with four open fires warming the welcoming bars. Old local photographs, brasses, a grandfather clock, mahogany and oak settles and other comfortable tables and chairs create the relaxed atmosphere that pervades here. Children are not allowed inside. Picnic tables outside.

On draught: Ansells Bitter, Boddingtons Bitter, Friary Meux Best Bitter, guest ale, Beamish, Guinness, Castlemaine XXXX, Wrexham lager, Lowenbrau, Addlestones cider.
Food: popular home-cooked meals include steak and kidney pie (£5), hot Madras-style prawns (£5), omelettes (£3.40-£4.60), rump steak (£7.95), filled

batches (from £1), lasagne, chilli (both £4), and daily specials. Treacle tart and home-made apple pie (£1.95) are popular desserts.

Times: 12-2pm and 7.30-9.30pm (10pm Fri and Sat). Telephone; 0352 740142.

∘━◆━◦

*F*rom the inn follow the road opposite, signposted A494 and Llanferres. Proceed downhill, then just before the road narrows by some cottages, take the footpath left into woodland above the river. On nearing a bridge, climb steps on the left and go uphill skirting woods and farmland to a road. Turn right downhill, cross a river bridge and climb uphill, then opposite houses on your left take the footpath into woodland, signposted Leete Path. It passes above a spectacular gorge, under some sheer rock faces by a deep chasm, where rock climbers practise, and near old caves where calcite was once mined. Disregard paths down to the river and eventually merge with the Loggerheads nature trail. Those with energy left can climb the steps that lead to the cliffs towering over the country park. Otherwise, keep on along the river bank back to the car park.

Mold
The county town of Clwyd, a busy market centre and the centre of the North Wales coalfield. Interesting features are the picturesque High Street and the 15th-century church with its remarkable fresco painting of animals.

ℋANTER HILL ~to~ 𝒪LD RADNOR

APPROXIMATELY 5 MILES

A straightforward walk through rolling hill and farming countryside, close to the Offa's Dyke, Hergest Ridge and the English border.

Parking

OS Map 148 Ref SO2456. Park on the west side of B4594 in a broad forest entrance, 1 mile south of Dolyhir.

Harp Inn

Old Radnor, Presteigne - village signed off A44 Kington to New Radnor road.

FURTHER EXPLORATION

Old Radnor

The 14th-century church of St Stephen the Martyr, one of the finest in Wales, claims that its organ case (1500) is the oldest in Britain. The font is formed from what is believed to have been a Bronze Age altar stone.

*T*urn left down the road for 50 yards, then bear right through a gate by an old shed onto a track. Proceed uphill through two gates by a refurbished cottage, then shortly, at the end of a fence, turn left uphill to a gate. Turn right along the hedge, join a grassy footpath and at a junction of waymarked paths, turn left onto a footpath round Hanter Hill. Pass a white cottage, then close to the base of the hill, follow the hedge on your right to a metal gate by Rock Cottage and turn left along a metalled track to a road. Cross over, shortly to take a footpath left over a brook and bear right uphill to a gate. Turn immediately right over a wooden fence, bear left alongside a brook uphill to a stile and road. Turn right, pass Yatt Farm and some houses, then turn right in front of the church for the inn.

᥍*Harp Inn* (Free House)᥍

Peacefully set on a hillside with wonderful views overlooking the valley and Radnor Forest, this quaint 15th-century inn boasts antique furniture and a friendly atmosphere. Its beamed and flagstone-floored bars are warmed by open fires. Children and dogs are welcome; there is a separate restaurant area and three charming guest bedrooms are available. There is pleasant seating outside.

On draught: Whitbread's Welsh Bitter, Wood's Special Bitter, Wye Valley Hereford Supreme, guest ale, Tennants Pilsner, Carling Black Label, Scrumpy Jack cider and well priced wines.
Food: a short lunchtime menu includes ploughman's (£2.75), soup (£1.95), sandwiches (from £1.39) and lasgne (£3.95). Evening fare extends to chicken Kiev (£5.25), beef curry (£3.95), carbonade of beef (£4.95) and steaks (from £8.50).
Times: 12-2pm and 7-9pm. Telephone: 054421 655.

etrace your steps past the church, turn right, then in 50 yards left onto a road and pass a farm onto a track into a field. Turn left by the hedge, climb a stile by a large oak tree, then turn right along the hedge and go through a gate. Turn left, cross disused railway via two gates and continue to a gate and road. Turn right, then in 300 yards, left onto a track to Blacklands House and go through a gap in a conifer hedge to your right, beside the house. Proceed alongside a wall for 50 yards, go up a bank and turn right in a field to a stile. Cross a stream and stile on left, then follow an old sunken footpath and field edge to a gate and track. Continue through three gates to a road. Go left across the road, along a track and bear left in front of a farm to a T-junction. Turn right, pass the farm and take an arrowed path left. Cross a stream, bear left uphill, pass through a metal gate and bear half-left across a field to a stile into a wood. Continue until the path merges with a footpath from the left. Bear right, head downhill to a stile, then bear right across a field to a stile and road. Turn right for your car.

New Radnor

In spite of its name the village is 700 years old and has the ruins of a castle two centuries older. It is beautifully placed at the foot of the Radnor Forest which consists of rolling hills and a series of deep valleys, locally called 'dingles', which are haunts of badgers and other wildlife.

Kington

Sheltered by Hergest Ridge and Rushock Hill, Kington is famous for its sheep markets. Offa's Dyke, the old Mercian defence against the Welsh, crosses Rushock Hill to the north. A long-distance footpath now follows its line.

$\mathcal{B}$RECON ~to~ $\mathcal{L}$LANFRYNACH

APPROXIMATELY 6 MILES

A gentle, easy-to-follow walk mostly alongside the River Usk, and along the towpath to the Monmouthshire and Brecon Canal.

Parking

OS Map 160 Ref SO0428. In one of the several car parks in Brecon.

$\mathcal{L}$ocate the main road bridge to the south of the town, close to Christ College. Cross the bridge, immediately turn left along a lane beside the college and take the waymarked footpath through a gate to the left of a cottage. Follow the riverbank through a field, climb a stile, then cross a small bridge over a stream and turn left onto a track. Rejoin the footpath at a stile, continue beside the river, cross another stile and proceed along a narrow footpath through trees to a stile into a field. Head down the field and go through a tunnel under the road to a gate. Turn right and proceed to a stile at the edge of a wood. Turn left, then at a fork of paths, take the higher path and continue through a wide clearing between trees. Cross two stiles, then keep close to the right-hand hedge to a further stile. Follow the hedged footpath to a wooden bridge over the Afon Cynrig beside Abercynrig Mill. Cross the bridge, turn right and go through the gates at the side of the mill onto a grassy path between walls and then hedges onto a metalled track leading to a road. Cross over to a stile and take the signed footpath to St Brynach's Church and keep ahead for the inn.

———————◆◆◆◆◆———————

From the inn follow the footpath back past the church to the road. Turn right, then at a T-junction, turn left downhill to a bridge over the River Usk. Turn left along the canal towpath at Brynach Lock and follow the path to the end of the canal in Brecon. Proceed ahead for 50 yards and turn right back into the town to return to wherever you parked your car.

↷ *White Swan* (*Free House*) ↶

At the heart of the village, this 17th-century pub has a simple rustic bar featuring flagstone floors, rough stone walls, oak beams, a vast inglenook and comfortable alcove seating. In the friendly and relaxed atmosphere children and dogs are most welcome. Outside there is a charming, secluded rose and shrub-filled terrace.

On draught: Brains Bitter, Welsh Bitter, Flowers IPA, Guinness, Stella Artois, Strongbow, Woodpecker cider.
Food: emphasis on good home-cooked dishes including haddock and prawn pie (£6), Welsh-style grilled trout (£7.50), steaks (£8.90-£12.90), Swan smokie (£3.30), lamb chops marinated in garlic and herbs (£7.50), plus French onion soup (£2.35) and ploughman's (£4). Puddings (£1.95).
Times: 12-2pm and 7-9.30pm, (Sun 12-1.30pm and 7-9pm). Closed all day Mon, except Bank Hols. Telephone 087486 276.

White Swan

Llanfrynach, Brecon. The village is signposted from B4458, just off A40, east of the Brecon bypass.

FURTHER EXPLORATION

Brecon

An old market town of narrow streets, at the confluence of the Rivers Honddu and Usk, with many country crafts and antique shops, two notable museums, the ruins of a medieval castle and a partly 13th-century fortified cathedral. The cathedral contains a fine Norman font and the largest preserved cresset stone in Wales; the cresset was an ancient stone which had 30 cups containing oil for lighting the cathedral.

Tretower Court and Castle

The castle is a substantial ruin of an 11th-century motte and bailey, with a three-storey tower and 9ft thick walls. The court is a 14th-century fortified manor house, much extended and altered over the years. Open daily all year. Telephone: 0874 730279.

STOCKLEY WOOD ~to~ LLYSWEN

APPROXIMATELY 6 MILES

A scenic, peaceful walk through wood and farmland, using part of the delightful Wye Valley Walk, along one of Britain's most beautiful rivers.

Parking
OS Map 161 Ref SO1140.
Layby on the east side of A470, 900 yards north of the entrance to Llangoed Hall, north of Llyswen.

Griffin Inn
Llyswen, Brecon - on A470 Builth Wells to Brecon road.

FURTHER EXPLORATION

Hay-on-Wye
A small market town set above the River Wye, with the Black Mountains, at their steepest and grandest, looming nearby. Narrow streets winding through the old town are full of fascinating shops, especially book shops and on market day are alive with bustling activity.

Continue north along the A470, take the first road left and ascend to a white house - Cefngafros - on your right. Turn left uphill on a footpath through bracken, go through a gate onto a woodland track and continue uphill, turning right onto a track beyond an old wooden hut on your left. Take the second track round to the left, then shortly take the first track right and maintain direction to exit the wood via a metal gate. Continue ahead and pass through two gates to Llanfawr Farm. Keep the farm to your left, bear right along a track for 100 yards, then keep right again at a junction, following the track to a metal gate. Remain on the farm track round the field edge, cross a stream, go through the left of two metal gates and bear half-left across the next field to a gate in the corner. Follow the hedge left-handed to join a track and soon pass through Upper Llangoed farmyard, via two gates to a road. Turn right, then at a cattle grid just past a white house on the left, turn left onto a path through bracken beside a hedge. Shortly, bear left along a grassy hedged track and cross open ground to a gate and track into a wood. At a junction in a clearing, take the left-hand path across the clearing and descend to pass through a metal gate. Climb a metal stile, then cross the right-hand of two wooden stiles and continue directly ahead over three stiles, through a gate to join a track down to a road. Turn left for the pub.

$\backsim$*Griffin Inn* *(Free House)*$\backsim$

This 15th-century creeper-clad inn has two friendly bars, which boast a wealth of oak beams, good log fires, a stone-flagged floor and old fishing tackle in the public bar, with settles and various fishing trophies and pictures filling the comfortable lounge bar. Accommodation, fishing and shooting are available. Children and dogs are most welcome. Garden.

On draught: Boddingtons, Flowers IPA, Whitbread Best Bitter, Welsh Bitter, Guinness, Stella Artois, Heineken, Strongbow and Captain Major's Own cider.
Food: good hearty country cooking may include home-made cream of Stilton soup (£2.90), wild duck terrine (£3.95), ragoût of wild rabbit (£7.75), curry and rice (£6.25), mushroom and cheese pasta, shepherd's pie (both £4.50), roast Welsh lamb and mint sauce (£9.50), with lemon crunch or apple and whinberry crumble (£2.85) for pudding. Set Sunday lunch (£11.50). There is also a restaurant.
Times: 12-2pm and 7-9pm. Roast only Sun lunchtime; no food Sun evening (except residents). Telephone: 0874 754241.

---

*T*urn left from the inn, then after 300 yards turn right beside the Bridge End Inn. Beyond the school, turn left onto a lane, signed Llwybr Crhoeddus. Follow the lane and later a track past the Shrubbery, a Welsh Water complex, and through gates along the waymarked Wye Valley Walk, with the River Wye to your right, to a road. Turn left back to your car.

Llangoed Castle
A large mansion in 17th-century style, but rebuilt in 1912 by Clough Williams-Ellis, architect of the Italianate village of Portmeirion.

Maesyronnen Chapel
(five miles north-east of Llyswen, off A438). The chapel in this tiny hamlet was founded around 1696 and is one of the earliest places of worship for Nonconformists. It contains much original 18th- and 19th-century furniture.

ℋENLLAN ~to~ ℒLANTHONY

**APPROXIMATELY
4 MILES**

*A pleasant walk
through the Vale of
Ewyas, close to the
Afon Honddu with
splendid views of the
Black Mountains.*

Parking
OS Map 161 Ref SO2625. In a
layby 300 yards south of
Henllan.

Half Moon Inn
Llanthony, near Abergavenny.

FURTHER EXPLORATION

Llanthony Priory
In the early 12th century
William de Lacey founded the
priory on the site of a
hermitage dedicated to St
David which had been built
600 years earlier. Although the
first church on the site was
destroyed, a new one built in
the late 12th century makes
the picturesque ruin seen
today. Accessible all year.

ℋead south along the road for 650 yards to a waymarked stile beside a gate on the left. Bear half-left across a field to a bridge over the Afon Honddu, then turn left and follow waymarked stiles across fields to derelict farm buildings. Leave the farm via an arrowed stile and proceed across fields and further stiles to join a farm track. Continue to a stile in front of a farmyard, then follow the track uphill past farm buildings and proceed across waymarked stiles and through gateways to a stile and road. Turn right, enter Llanthony - bearing right if you wish to visit the old priory - and continue for a short distance to the Half Moon on your left.

✑Half Moon Inn (Free House)✑

Unpretentious and unspoilt, this village inn has a warm welcome for walkers in its small stone-walled and flag-floored bar where a wood-burning stove ensures comfort. Children are welcome inside, and there is a separate dining room. Overnight accommodation is available.

On draught: Hook Norton Best Bitter, Welsh Bitter, Budweiser, Heineken, Bulmers Traditional cider.
Food: a good choice of snacks and meals include sandwiches (£1.25), home-made soup (£2), ploughman's (£3.30-£3.80), plaice and scampi (£4.50), chicken curry (£4.30).
Times: 12-2pm and 6-8.30pm (from 7pm Sun).
Telephone: 0873 890611.

𝒯urn left from the inn, take the first turning left across two bridges over streams and proceed uphill. In 200 yards, turn left through a gate onto a

track and continue through further gates to Cym Bwchel Farm. Turn right in front of the farm, head steeply uphill to a stile and continue uphill to a further stile, then take the waymarked path to Sunny Bank. Walk downhill, cross a stream, then turn left along a footpath around the hillside - fine views of Llanthony Priory and the hills beyond - to join a track. Pass a cottage on your right, go through a gate, then at a fork bear right, following the track past another cottage to a junction of tracks. Keep right, pass through a gate, then in 200 yards where the track bears right uphill, take a grassy path down to and across a stream. Go through a gate and turn left down to a gate through a farmyard. Bear right, then left through a further gate and continue ahead down a track to a road. Turn right and you will have about 300 yards to walk back to your car in the layby.

Vale of Ewyas
The narrow road that runs through this valley, flanked on the east by the Black Mountains, is the most direct - if not the quickest - route between Hay-on-Wye and Abergavenny. The Offa's Dyke footpath, marking the English border, crosses the hills above the Vale.

ᴛWEEDSMUIR KIRK~to~ᴄROOK INN

*The outward walk
undulates through
forest along the side of
the Tweed Valley and
around deep gullies,
affording fine views.
The route returns
along the river bank.*

Parking
OS Map 71 Ref NT 1024.
Tweedsmuir Kirk car park, off
A701 at Newbiggin.

Crook Inn
Tweedsmuir. On A701 Moffat
to Edinburgh road, a mile north
of Tweedsmuir.

ᴌeave the car park, going back up the gravel track, bearing left onto a narrow tarmac road. Cross a stone bridge, go through a metal gate and just beyond the sheep fold bear right up to the Forestry gate. Cross the disused railway and continue to climb around the edge of Cockiland Hill to a fork. Descend left, cross a concrete bridge and ascend around Whiteside Rig. Proceed around the end of Moat Burn, and Hog Hill to Hearthstane Burn. Go through the gate and follow the electric fence down to the burn, crossing the fence by the stile at the bottom. Cross the burn by the plank bridge, and go up the bank to rejoin the track going down through Hearthstane Farm. Follow the drive over the Tweed to the A701, turning right for the Inn.

ᴄ*Crook Inn* (Free House)ᴄ

Dating back to 1604 the Crook Inn is Scotland's oldest licensed inn. The atmospheric bar, with associations with Robert Burns, has flagged floors and an open fire. An extension furnished in Art-Deco style overlooks the Tweed and has eight bedrooms. Children welcome.
On draught: Broughton Greenmantle Ale, McEwan 80/-, Tartan Special, Guinness, Dry Blackthorn cider.
Food: good value dishes include soup (£1.50), smoked trout mousse (£3.25), ploughman's (£3.50), steak pie (£5.50), mixed grill (£10.50) and chicken curry (£4.95).
Times: 12-9pm, restaurant 7-9pm. Bar open 11am-11pm (12.30pm Sun). Telephone: 08997 272.

ᴡalk back along A701, turn left over the Tweed towards Hearthstane Farm and right before the farm by a lamp-post past the first house. Go along the track, through fields and gates to a wall. Turn right along the wall to the river and keep along the bank between river and wall. Cross a burn via a plank, go under a disused railway bridge, rejoin outward pat, just before a sheep fold. Cross river back to your car.

LOCH OF LOWES ~to~ TIBBIE SHIELS INN

ross the road to the track signposted to Sca Cleuch and Ettrick Kirk and Riskinhope Farm. On reaching the bridge over Little Yarrow, leave the track to follow the river to the loch. Turn right along the shore as far as the fence at the corner of the loch by the wooded area. Cross the gate and ascend the bank to pick up the narrow path above the loch, just below the telegraph line. As it descends the other end by a forestry area, fork left through a lift-up gate and cross a field to a flat bridge over a burn and onto the gate at the far end of the field. Turn right down the tarmac road to the inn.

Tibbie Shiels Inn (Free House)

An 18th-century whitewashed cottage beautifully situated in six acres overlooking the loch.The friendly, atmospheric bar has low ceilings and open fires. There is also a restaurant extension with five letting bedrooms. Children are welcome and there is good seating outside in summer. No dogs are permitted.
On draught: Broughton Greenmantle Ale, Bellhaven 80/-, bottled strong Traquair Ale, range of malt whiskies. **Food:** good selection of home-cooked meals range from soup (£1.50), Yarrow trout (£4.50) and spicy chicken (£3.75) to steak and kidney pudding (£4.50) and clootie dumpling (£1.70) for pudding. High tea (£7.50).
Times: 12.30-2.30 and 6.30-8.30pm, High teas 3.30-6pm. Closed Mon, Nov to Feb. Bar open 11am-11pm, Sun from noon. Telephone: 0750 42231.

urn right out of the inn, back up the tarmac road, over the stone bridge straddling the connecting stream between Loch of Lowes and St Mary's Loch, to the main road. Turn left and walk along the loch roadside back to the car.

APPROXIMATELY 3 MILES

An attractive, easy walk along the lochside hill path with an ever changing sky and loch reflections and splendid landscape views.

Parking
OS Map 79 Ref NT2318. Layby on A708 Moffat to Selkirk road, south of Loch Lowes.

Tibbie Shiels Inn
St Mary's Loch, Selkirk - 100 yards off A708, 13 miles west of Selkirk.

FURTHER EXPLORATION

Isabella 'Tibbie' Shiels moved into what was then St Mary's Cottage in 1823 with her molecatcher husband. She began to take in lodgers and guests - including famous literary figures - after her husband's death in order to support her large family and successfully ran the business for over 75 years, until her death in 1878, aged 98.

$\mathcal{C}$OLVEND ~to~ $\mathcal{K}$IPPFORD

**APPROXIMATELY
6 MILES**

*This walk offers a
wide range of scenery,
from forest track and
open heathland to
coastal path and
fishing village.
Generally level with
steady climbs in and
out of Kippford.*

Start of Walk
OS Map 84 Ref 8654. Colvend
village hall on the A710
Dalbeattie to Dumfries road.

Anchor Hotel
Quayside, Kippford, near
Dalbeattie. Off A710, 4 miles
south of Dalbeattie.

From the village hall take the path at the eastern end serving houses, and leading to Dalbeattie Forest. Proceed through the forestry fence onto the defined path leading to Barean Loch. Continue past the loch for just over 500 yards, then bear left onto a grassy path across heathland and through gates to a farmhouse. Cross the forecourt, go through a gate onto a single-track tarmac road, following it to A710. Cross over, go through a green gate onto a track towards Mark Hill. At a wide clearing follow the signpost right for Kippford which takes you up round the Scaur (fine hill views and eventually glimpses of the Solway inlet of Rough Firth). Follow the path down around the back of houses, and the Lifeboat station to Kippford quayside with its profusion of yachts and boats. Turn right for the Anchor Hotel.

❧*Anchor Hotel* *(Free House)*❧

Prettily set, this harbourside pub faces a quiet yacht anchorage with splendid views across the Firth from the comfortably furnished lounge bar. The old-fashioned, wood-panelled public bar has kept a seafaring atmosphere and is the place where the local fishermen and yachting folk congregate. There is also a games room and in warm weather customers can sit outside. Children are welcome.

On draught: McEwan 80/-, Theakston Best Bitter and Old Peculier, Guinness, Becks Bier.
Food: the bar menu and daily specials may offer steak (£8.65), fish (from £4), salads (£3.85-£5.20), vegetarian meals (from £3.75) and puddings like American fudge cake (£2.10). Children's menu (£1.85).
Times: 12-9pm (Jun to Aug), 12-2pm and 6-9pm (Sep to May). Open 9.30am-mdnt (Jun to Aug); 9.30am-2.30pm and 6-11pm (Sep to May). Telephone: 055662 205.

---

*R*etrace your steps along the quayside to the Post Office, bearing left up a winding tarmac road, signposted 'Jubilee Footpath to Rockcliffe 1 mile'. Admiring the heather garden in Dorus Mhor, proceed up a well defined stony path. Routes off this main path offer some interesting views. Pursuing the main path, however, pass Baron's Craig Hotel, picking up a narrow tarmac road leading down to right into the attractive estuary of Rockcliffe and Port Donnet with its sandy coves and rocky outcrops. Climb out of Rockcliffe on the road to Colvend, following it for one and a quarter miles to the main road. Turn right to get back to the village hall.

FURTHER EXPLORATION

Kippford
A small yachting and bathing resort. On the hill-walk to the neighbouring village of Rockliffe is the Mote of Mark, a pre-Roman hill-fort overlooking the coast and a bird sanctuary on Rough Island. This was a smuggling coastline; in the 18th century, wines and tobacco were smuggled into the inlets of the Solway Firth to escape increased import duties.

Orchardton Tower
Palnackie (6 miles south-east of Castle Douglas)
John Cairns built this rare example of a circular tower in the late 15th century. Open at all reasonable times.

Threave Castle
Castle Douglas
Built by Archibald the Grim in the late 14th century, this lonely castle stands on an islet in the River Dee. Open daily Apr to Sep.

Threave Garden
Castle Douglas
Over 200 varieties of daffodil can be seen in spring in these fascinating gardens which house the National Trust for Scotland's School of Horticulture. There is something of interest at every season. Open daily all year. Telephone: 0556 2575.

CRINAN CANAL WALK

APPROXIMATELY 6 MILES

A flat, easy walk along the wide path of the Crinal Canal through changing scenery of open country, marshland and views of Loch Crinan and surrounding hills.

Parking

OS Map 55 Ref 8290. Dunardy Forest Walk car park, on B841, off A816 2 miles north of Lochgilphead.

Crinan Hotel

Crinan, near Lochgilphead. At the end of B841 north-east of Lochgilphead.

*H*ead back down the gravel access road and bear left on B841. Pass a house, then pick up a path towards the canal and cross the footbridge at Lock 10. Turn left along the towpath. At Dunardy Bridge keep left alongside the canal, go through a metal gate, past locks and continue to Bellanoch Lock and cross B8025. Note the yacht basin (left). Pass through a white gate marked 'Private Road. BWB Private Vehicles Only' and shortly bear right then steadily round left as you begin to see Crinan Loch with glimpses of the Sound of Jura, Craignish Point and the tip of Jura itself. Cross Lock 14 onto the access road, going either left into the coffee shop, or right, up the hill to the hotel.

⇔*Crinan Hotel* (Free House)⇔

An imposing Victorian building in the Scottish baronial style overlooking the sea, with stunning views from both the lounges and public bar. There are a roof-top bar, a coffee shop by Lock 14, two restaurants (smart dress expected), a family room and guest bedrooms.

On draught: Tennent 70/- and 80/-, Guinness, lager. **Food:** popular bar meals feature home-made soup (£1.60), fresh fish - Loch Craignish mussels (£5.25), Loch Awe trout (£4.65). Snacks and teas are served in the coffee shop. Restaurant menus are more expensive **Times:** 11am-11pm; winter 11am-2.30pm and 5-11pm. Coffee shop Apr to mid Sep. Seafood restaurant Tue to Sat 8pm, May to Sep, Westwood Room all year 7-9pm.

*B*efore setting off for the return walk, a rewarding diversion is to climb the Countryside Commission path from Lock 14, up to the heights overlooking Crinan and the Sound. Retrace your steps back along the canal to the car park remembering to come off the path and cross to the road at Lock 10.

ACHARN ~to~ KENMORE

*G*o up the track marked 'Falls of Acharn'. At the falls follow the sign to Hermit's Cave. Pass through the cave, continue uphill, then cross the bridge over the gorge. Bear right, follow the line of the gorge, then bear left, up to, then alongside, a fenced field. At an iron gate with a barn on the left, go through, and on to a T-junction. Pass through gates, cross a footbridge into a field, bear left with the line of the gorge, then right across a planked crossing beside a wire fence. Go round the farmhouse, leaving it to your left. Eventually, pass through a six-bar gate, climb two ladder stiles to reach a road. Turn left, descend, pass through a gate and go steeply down to A827. Cross over, and cross Loch Isthmus into Kenmore.

APPROXIMATELY 5 MILES

A delightful scenic walk passing the Falls of Acharn onto the hills high above Loch Tay, providing fine views across the valley. A few steep climbs with an easy return walk along the Loch.

Parking:
OS Map 51 Ref 8320. Parking area by road and sign to Acharn Falls, just beyond Acharn village on the south side of Loch Tay.

⇔Kenmore Hotel *(Free House)*⇔

This claims to be Scotland's oldest inn, and is set in a lovely village at the tip of Loch Tay. The Poet's Parlour bar, devoted to Burns, is cosy with a roaring log fire;. Archie's Bar is simpler but has a beautiful view of the river. Children welcome. Riverside garden.
On draught: Bellhaven 80/-, Beamish,
Food: menu includes pâté with oatcakes, avocado pear and garlic mushrooms (all £2.50), haddock, beef and Guinness pie and spaghetti (all about £5.50). Teas and sandwiches are available all day.
Times (bar meals): 12-2.30pm (2pm winter) and 7-9.30pm (9pm winter). Snacks all day. Open 11am (12.30pm Sun)-11.30pm. Telephone: 0887 830205.

Kenmore Hotel,
Kenmore . On A827 between Aberfeldy and Killin.

*R*etrace your steps across Loch Isthmus and bear right onto the lane along the loch shore. Pass Croft-na-Caber outdoor centre, and keep through Acharn to your car.

⚓COUNTY INDEX OF PUBS⚓